# VICTORIA PARK
# 100 YEARS OF A PARK & ITS PEOPLE

*An Historical and Photographic Essay On
Victoria Park, Kitchener, Ontario...
with Illuminations on the Neglected Past and Projected Future...*


*Prepared to Coincide with Victoria Park's Centennial
by rych mills
and the Victoria Park 100th Birthday Historical Committee
– Kitchener 1996 –*

Twin City Dwyer Printing Co. Ltd.: Official Printer of the Victoria Park 100th Birthday Committee

Published by the Victoria Park 100th Birthday Historical Committee
(Victoria Park Pavilion 80 Schneider Ave. Kitchener, Ontario  N2G 4G7)
Created in 1991 under the auspices of Kitchener Parks & Recreation

Text & photos printed by Twin City Dwyer Printing Co.Ltd.
Book Layout & Design by Lisa Schropp of Lisa's Loft Creations, Waterloo, Ontario
Typeface: Times, Regular, Italic, Bold, Extended
Paper: Bravo Dull
Cover Design by Peter Etril Snyder & Lisa Schropp
based on Peter Etril Snyder's 1995 painting "Winter Memories"... Victoria Park in the 1950s

We gratefully acknowledge funding assistance for this publication from

Waterloo Regional Heritage Foundation             Walter Bean             Canada Trust

# INTRODUCTION

*Nicholas Hill MLA OALA*
*Landscape Architect*

My first experience of Kitchener's Victoria Park was in the summer of 1995. I remember the day well. It was clear and sunny, about mid-morning. The lake reflected the clouds above. A slight mist softened the atmosphere. Subtle scents of flowers and shrubs drifted by. I was awe-struck by the quiet beauty and serenity of the Park. I felt I had been transported back to a Romantic Landscape of 18th century England.

Upon further study my first wonderful impressions of Victoria Park indeed proved largely correct – this is a park in the great 18th century Romantic Landscape tradition. It is with much pleasure, therefore, that I write this introduction to rych mills' **Victoria Park – 100 Years of a Park and Its People**, because it is, I suggest, one of the finest civic parks in our nation. But first let us ponder the development of parks in 19th century Ontario and the context for this park. Until the enactment of the Public Parks Act in 1883, public parks in Ontario were few. There was little need. Unlike Europe and the United States, our cities were relatively small and quite spacious. The civic park was more an idea than a pressing reality. Yet, curiously, the 40 year span between 1880 and 1920 was a golden period of park creation and Victoria Park stands out as one of the finest examples.

The earliest parks were often former military or federal lands which were given to a municipality for use as public open space. Parks also sometimes originated as cemeteries, which through disuse were converted to parks. The first true public parks in Ontario were established in Niagara-on-the-Lake, Toronto, Kingston and Hamilton. Often referred to as pleasure grounds, they were used primarily on summer evenings and Sundays when "people would spend the entire day in the park – with friends and books, watching squirrels and birds, listening to music, picnicking, playing croquet, boating, and watching their children play."[1] Each municipality had its reasons for establishing a park: civic pride, urban beautification, providing a place for active recreation and a strong moral conviction that nature refreshed and enhanced the body and soul.

The designs of these early parks was greatly influenced by an American, Francis Law Olmsted (1822-1903). Recognized as the father of landscape architecture, Olmsted promoted a natural character for the urban park, with a gentle landform, trees and water. This was considered a desirable contrast to city streets and structures. He was, in fact, continuing a landscape tradition founded in 18th century England that nature should be beautiful and picturesque. It is within this tradition and influenced by Olmsted's work that Victoria Park in the Town of Berlin, now the City of Kitchener, was born.

For me the triumph of Victoria Park is simply its beautiful landscape, based on the 18th century Romantic Landscape style. The characteristics of this style are experienced as one walks through the Park and include a naturalized character, with an emphasis on plantings and gentle landforms; sweeps of grass that provide openness and prospect; woods that provide shelter and enclosure to open areas; meandering paths and drives leading from one landscape 'picture' to another; 'antique' buildings and monuments that provide visual drama and historical associations; and vistas that extend the perception of the Park beyond its boundaries.

Stewardship of Victoria Park over the succeeding century has remained remarkably faithful to these original landscape ideals. The soul of the Park remains in its naturalness. Let us be sure to conserve and enhance this natural character for the next 100 years.

# "...GROUND ENOUGH
# TO COVER OUR BODIES..."

We celebrate 100 years of Victoria Park, a century of excitement and entertainment and events that go beyond the footnotes of history. We also celebrate the reverence felt by Aboriginal people for this particular site. That reverence was based on the land's dominating feature, a swamp. The presence of the original swamp also meant that the site remained undeveloped, remained available in 1894 when a new park was being planned. Victoria Park is today in the centre of a city of 200,000 because of that swampland.

A bronze plaque provides a spiritual link between today's Victoria Park and the time, centuries ago, when the land's life-giving ability meant survival for its earliest peoples.

The link is there. We treasure Victoria Park today, but Aboriginals and later natives treasured the site long before Kitchener, before Berlin, before the Schneiders, before the Ebys.

❧

In the 17th century, southern Ontario was home to Aboriginal natives including the Huron confederacy in the area around Georgian Bay and Lake Simcoe. Farther south, between the Huron and the Iroquois of New York State lived people whom the early French missionaries called the Neutrals. The Huron called the Neutrals 'Attiwandaronk' meaning 'people who speak a slightly different language.'[2]

Aboriginal life particularly pertinent to Victoria Park is documented in Ontario archaeologist David Boyle's 1894-95 report. Accompanied by Berlin's pre-eminent amateur historian, Jacob Stroh, Boyle travelled along a branch of Schneider Creek parallel to Strange Street as far as Glasgow Street. In the vicinity of the later Dominion Rubber/Uniroyal factory, they discovered evidence of a major Attiwandaronk village dating from the mid 1600s.

"Although cultivation has to a large extent levelled the banks surrounding...enough remains to show that they formed a large semi-circle enclosing about four acres, the ends running to a small trout stream flowing through a swamp close by...wild fruit was abundant including plums, cherries and huckleberries, and butter-nuts, beech-nuts and hazel-nuts grew in profusion."

Approximately 1,000 people would have wintered here with the population shrinking in summer as groups travelled far afield. Despite Boyle's plea that "...Berlin and Waterloo might...secure these fields for park purposes and thus aid in preserving a pre-historic monument..." nothing was done. All that remains of Boyle's evidence is that small trout stream. It is the eastern branch of Schneider Creek, crossing Gage, Cherry and Victoria Streets and flowing into Victoria Park. One hundred years ago, some of that swamp which Boyle mentioned was still evident at the western end of the park.[3]

❧

The Attiwandaronk declined substantially through the 1600s. A series of fatal epidemics, especially smallpox, devastated a population which had little immunity to European diseases. Iroquois-versus-Attiwandaronk warfare also played no small role in reducing each side's numbers. As the Ojibway of northern Ontario began moving south in the 18th century there was little opposition.[4]

When European and American settlers first arrived around 1800, Waterloo Township was a small part of the vast Ojibway nation covering much of Ontario and extending into the prairies. Within this Ojibway, or Anishnabeck, nation, the Mississaugas of the Credit River (now New Credit Reserve) managed the land and its resources from the shores of Lakes Erie and Ontario to the northern headwaters of the Thames, Grand, Humber and Rouge Rivers.

Mississauga camps differed greatly from those of their Attiwandaronk predecessors. The Mississaugas favoured campsites along major rivers during non-winter months and Doon, where Schneider Creek empties into the Grand River, was one such location.[5] Instead of large numbers living in villages, much smaller groups joined together in spring and summer. As colder months approached small bands would retreat into the heavily-forested parts of their territory. These small bands, often family-based, searched out locations with a good water supply, plenty of firewood and bountiful fish and game. Swamps, such as the one located where present-day Victoria Park stands, provided just such a combination.

From Doon, an Aboriginal trail paralleled Schneider Creek right up to the campsite on Strange Street. Generations of natives used this path, seeking winter villages and campgrounds. The trail passed directly through Victoria Park and the swamp at the park's western edge lured Mississaugas for many years. A swamp in winter could mean survival, could provide life. The arrival of settlers from America and Europe doomed the Mississauga way of life. In a provocative conclusion to his 1995 study, *"Mississauga Mennonite Relations in the Upper Grand River Valley"* E Reginald Good says:

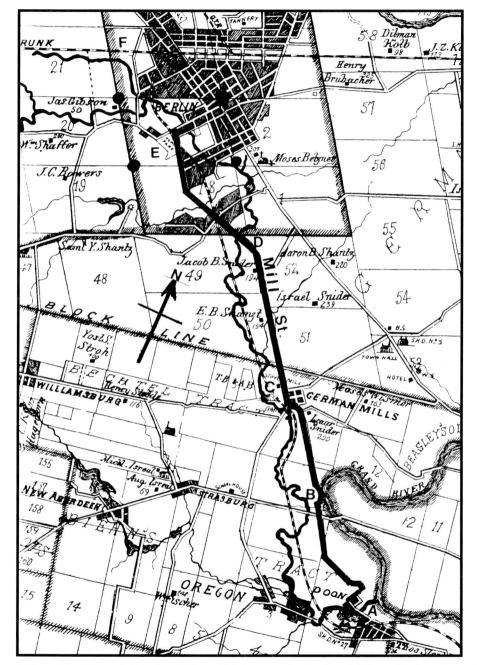

"Mennonites also collectively participated in depriving the Mississaugas of a land base...to reduce the Mississaugas to poverty and dependence...in forcing the Mississaugas out of their community and out of their historical memory."[6]

One of the small bands which maintained a modified form of the old way of life was the extended family of Tuhbenahneequay (Sarah Jones, 1780-1873). She is the focus of the Victoria Park plaque.

Tuhbenahneequay's band was the last of the New Credit Mississaugas to winter in what eventually became Victoria Park. This continued even after Joseph Schneider purchased and settled on the land in 1807. Each winter Tuhbenahneequay and family would appear along the trail and put up their camp near that same swamp which had so benefitted the Attiwandaronk centuries earlier. Tuhbenahneequay converted to Methodism in 1824 but maintained many Mississauga ways throughout her 93 years of life. It is said she never once slept in a bed, preferring a simple blanket on the ground. Two of her sons became among the best-known Mississaugas of their time.

Maungwudas (George Henry) was fully self-taught and spent many years working with the Wesleyan Missionary Society. He is also remembered as part of a later native dance troupe which entertained royalty and enthusiastic crowds on both sides of the Atlantic.

The more famous son is Kahkewaquonaby (Peter Jones). Raised within his mother's extended family, he experienced the fast-disappearing Mississauga lifestyle first-hand. His father was English, the well-known Ontario surveyor, Augustus Jones. Through him, Peter Jones learned the white man's ways. When the Mississaugas converted to Methodism in the 1820s, Peter Jones became a leading minister in the church. In several books, written late in life, he provided detailed accounts of the Mississauga experience which by then had all but disappeared. In addition to vivid descriptions, Kahkewaquonaby naturally laments the loss of his boyhood traditions. An 1845 passage still touches the heart with its truth: "...in a few years we will hardly have space enough left to lay down our bones upon, or ground enough to cover our bodies...."[7]

It is through this mother and two sons, commemorated on the Victoria Park plaque, that a door opens on life in the Schneider Creek area before the white man's invasion changed it forever.

*The original route of Mill Street from Doon to Berlin followed closely the Aboriginal trail paralleling Schneider Creek. This extract from an 1881 map of Waterloo Township traces the route. A) is the Schneider Creek outlet into the Grand River where Mississaugas often gathered in summer and fall. B) is the site of Homer Watson Park and Doon Heritage Crossroads. C) German Mills was an important milling community, since swallowed up by Kitchener. It is slightly north of Manitou and Bleams. D) is the present site of Rockway Golf Course. E) is located just west of the Town Park (Woodside). The four black dots around E are the corners of Joseph Schneider's Lot 17. F) is the approximate site of the Aboriginal village south of the corner of Strange Street and Glasgow. The present Mill Street in Kitchener ends at D. Its original route is approximated by Carwood, Vanier and part of Manitou. The roadway at B, in Homer Watson Park is closed to traffic but when walked gives some idea of what the old trail must have been like. The word BERLIN is printed where Victoria Park was later built. Much of the land from the B in BERLIN up to F was swamp in pre 20th century times*

*William Crabb's portrait of Kahkewaquonaby is the frontispiece to the 1861 edition of 'History of the Ojebway Indians.' The book is one of the most detailed records available of the transition from native lifestyle to white man's. Maungwudas' recollections of his dance troupe's visit to Europe appear in an 1848 booklet 'An Account of the Chippewa Indians who have been Travelling among the Whites....' This is a much rarer publication and is one of the first impressions of travel abroad by a native North American. Chippewa is the American term for Ojibway. Ojebway is a mid 19th century spelling.[8]*

*On a prominent pathway in Victoria Park a plaque commemorating native use of the surrounding land was unveiled on October 11, 1992. At the ceremony Clara Prince and Terry Rogers hold the traditionally designed leather cover which had shielded the plaque. The memorial was installed by the 1992 Group, a coalition of local organizations providing an alternative view during the 500th anniversary of the white man's landing on 'Turtle Island.' (North America).*

The same flowing stream, the same swampy terrain, the same forests which made the Victoria Park area so important to the Attiwandaronk and Mississaugas also made it important to Joseph Schneider in 1807 when he first saw his recently-purchased land, Lot 17. It is no accident that his still-standing 1816 house sits equidistant from that ancient Aboriginal pathway (which became Mill Street) and Lot 17's principal waterway (which became Schneider Creek).

The Mississauga concept of land *stewardship* was fundamentally at odds with the settlers' land *ownership* and the outcome was predictable. E Reginald Good states, after many years of study, "...Mississaugas virtually disappear from the historical record after 1840...."[9]

That there was more to native and pioneer relationships than conflict and displacement is evidenced in a treasured vignette from the Schneider family. W V Uttley's tribute to the Schneiders, which appeared in the 1929 edition of the Waterloo Historical Society Report,

*In King William IV's name, the government presented all recognized chiefs in Canada with the 'Chief's Medal.' This one underlines the important role Peter Jones/Kahkewaquonaby played in the two worlds of Upper Canada/Southern Ontario. The translation of native names into English spelling is still not an exact science. In English, Kahkewaquonaby means Sacred Waving Feather while Maungwudas translates as Great Hero or Big Legging.[10]*

contains recollections by Louisa Troxell (1847-1936) a daughter of Joseph E and Sarah Schneider. Using the language of his day, Uttley wrote:

"She remembers the time when the Indians used to call at her father's home on New Year's day and bring gifts of beads, baskets, and other handmade things. When they entered the house she used to hide behind her mother's skirts, yet every now and then peep at them. The fearful-looking red men would not, however, depart until they had received presents in exchange for their own. Her mother, who was kindhearted always gave them more than she received, in the form of food and cloth."[11]

A New Year's Day gift exchange near Victoria Park, circa 1855![12]

## "...WHERE ONCE WERE FIELDS..."

Susan Burke
Curator, Joseph Schneider Haus Museum

How could one presume to imagine how the Schneiders felt on that June day in 1807 when they first glimpsed the land that was to be their new Canadian home. The journey from Lancaster County, Pennsylvania had been a long one, and arduous. The four wagons that hauled their possessions and those of fellow Mennonites in their party, the Benjamin Ebys, the Peter Erbs, Abraham Weber and several other families, were overloaded and the women had had to walk the greater part of the way. Moreover, the company had encountered poor road conditions and numerous delays. So it was likely with joy and great relief that Joseph, Barbara and their four children contemplated their new purchase and set about exploring the property to choose a site for their first dwelling.

Joseph was probably not surprised by what he encountered on Lot 17 of the German Company Tract. His older brother Jacob (Yoch) had explored the area on horseback two years earlier and had returned to Pennsylvania with enthusiastic reports. A year later in 1806, Jacob and another brother,

Christian, had made the long trek with their families to settle in Waterloo Township and Joseph's brother-in-law Benjamin Eby was also in the area "inspecting the nature of the country in which their relatives had so largely invested."[13] He too, purchased land, Lot 2, adjacent to Lot 17 where his sister Barbara and brother-in-law Joseph Schneider would settle a year later.

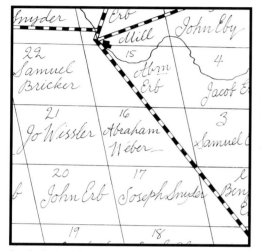

*Detail of a hand-drawn map of Waterloo Township (ca 1820). This map shows Joseph Schneider's 448 acre farm (Lot 17) and Benjamin Eby's property (Lot 2) bisected by the Great Road (now King Street) which proceeds in a westerly direction towards the mill (now Waterloo) where it turns north.*

What Joseph Schneider did encounter that summer's day was virgin timber – cedar, maple and white pine, some trees on the farm described later by granddaughter Louisa as being six feet in diameter. There were some low swampy areas and to the north in the direction of Ben Eby's, rolling hills of sandy soil. About a quarter mile south of the 'Great Road' (now King Street), a rivulet of sparkling water drained a large swamp and meandered through his property. It was near the banks of this stream, close to a natural spring, that Joseph built their first dwelling. This modest one storey log cabin, located not far from where Barra Castle stands today, was home to the Schneiders for close to a decade.[14] Those first years were difficult ones, marked by back-breaking manual labour. Trees were cleared, stumps removed, crops planted. But the Schneiders were industrious and before the first decade was out, sixty acres of Joseph's 448 acre farm had been cleared, Schneider's Road had been cut northward to meet the Great Road, and he was constructing his second house.[15]

The commodious Georgian home he built, this time on the opposite side of the creek, was reminiscent of the Mennonite farm homes in the rolling farmland near Manheim, Pennsylvania, where he grew up. And like those Pennsylvania-German farmsteads, other small outbuildings designed to perform specific functions were added over the years so that granddaughter Louisa described the farm as "looking like a village." Located on the creek side of the house was the wash house, a spring house for refrigeration and a brick building housing a bake oven, meat smoking compartment and a

chamber for drying fruits and vegetables. A large bank barn in the Pennsylvania-German style was located to the south of the farmhouse approximately where Queen Street meets Schneider Avenue today. To the west was the original apple orchard, a few trees from which were still standing when the first house on Schneider Avenue was built by Joseph's grandson, David, in 1888.

Pennsylvania-German farmers were wise to isolate auxiliary activity areas in well-separated buildings as the risk of fire was ever-present. The Schneiders were lucky. Their wood-frame house still stands today after a hundred and eighty years in spite of the fact that fire destroyed their nearby barn in 1873.[16]

Like many of his Mennonite co-religionists, Joseph Schneider had a secondary trade which he combined with farming; he had a sawmill. It is unclear when he constructed this mill but he began to be assessed for it in the 1820s. To provide a great enough head of water to power his overshot wheel, Joseph dammed Schneider Creek near the railway tracks where they now pass the park limits. A long mill race directed the water to the mill which he located behind the farmstead approximately where 129 David Street stands today near Roland.[17]

*Detail from a bird's-eye view of Berlin, Ontario, Canada in 1875 showing the Schneider farm with its outbuildings which, to Louisa, resembled a villiage. Note the location of the sawmill and mill pond, the first barn (near Schneider Avenue today) and the bridge where Schneider Creek passed under Schneider Road (now Queen Street South). Mill Street and the Galt Branch of the Grand Trunk Railway intersect Schneider Road at left.*

The operation of the sawmill meshed naturally with the level of the water in the creek and with seasonal farm routines. Sawing was impossible during the three coldest months and when the water was low in July but other times of the year the mill was busy and business brisk. In the early years, the Schneiders realized considerable income from the sawmill; the mill provided lumber for the building of shops and homes and when the railway arrived in 1856, the sale of cordwood for firing the engines became quite lucrative.

However, Schneider's water-powered mill gradually succumbed to competition from more efficient steam-powered operations. As forests were cleared and wetlands drained, former regular supplies of water dwindled into flows for shorter periods. Timber became scarce and by the 1870s the rumble of the mill wheel was heard no more. Louisa remembers the large wheel standing long after the sawmill itself had tumbled down.

For the first two generations of Schneiders, life centred around the farmhouse and the mill, and the waters of the creek which bear their name was truly a life force. Joseph's son, Joseph E and his wife Sarah Shantz raised nine more children on its banks and it is this third generation which best records the environment which was to become the town's new park.

*It was the children of the second generation of Schneiders to live in the homestead, who describe most accurately their physical environment that was to become Victoria Park. David (left), Samuel (right) and Louisa (back row left) also lived in the vicinity as adults. This photograph was taken in 1907.*

Sons David (1840-1928) and Samuel (1842-1912) describe long work days ploughing as far north as St George and David Streets and sawing, sometimes until after midnight when the water was high. Daughter Louisa recalls her mother helping to wash the sheep in the creek before the spring shearing as well as laundering their own clothes there before the family wash house was constructed. Geese were kept on the flats and Sarah would pluck a rich harvest of down from them, live, every six weeks, to assure a constant supply of feathers for pillows and featherbeds. On the occasions when playtime was permitted, the Schneider children, as children will, gravitated to the creek. They loved to fish in the well-stocked mill pond and race while tumbles into the water were reportedly frequent. When swimming became popular, the village boys joined the Schneider boys at the "old swimming hole", that part of the mill race where David Street is today.

But the first Mennonite settlers in the area were serious farmers and the Schneiders were no exception. When a newcomer named Varnum knocked on their door in the early 1820s wanting to buy a piece of land near the Great Road for a blacksmith shop and roadhouse, Joseph was hesitant. Though his property had sand hills and swampy areas which couldn't be farmed, still his land was his fortune. Realizing the importance of the availability of a skilled blacksmith, however, he leased Varnum a small lot where Schneider's Road met the Great Road, today, the corner of King and Queen Streets where the Walper stands. The growth around this essential service of the village which was to become Berlin, is now history.

Joseph apparently remained reluctant to sell off much farmland in spite of the demands of the growing village. After his death in 1844, the farm still comprised 324 acres. In like manner, son Joseph E resisted the temptation to "strike it rich" when the Grand Trunk Railway brought development to adjacent properties in the early 1850s. Abraham C Weber, on neighbouring Lot 16, through which the rail line would pass, sold his complete farm for $60 an acre, gaining millionaire status in many people's eyes. The building lots surveyed from this farmland for George John Grange, a speculator from Guelph, stop abruptly at Schneider's Lot 17, forming an oblique line on the map which survives today as the northwestern boundary of Victoria Park.[18]

*This map of 1853-54 shows the lots surveyed for George John Grange that abut the boundary of the Schneider farm, preserved today, in part, as the northwestern limit of Victoria Park. At this time, two large portions of the ancient swamp were still prominent enough to merit being named, Cedar Swamp and Black Ash Swamp. In 1996, despite complete urbanization, remnants of the swamp remain evident in Cherry Park.*

As Joseph E grew older, his enthusiasm for farming diminished and he concentrated his energies on the sawmill, turning over the operation of the farm to his two sons Samuel and David. More lots were sold off including 25 acres of sandy-soiled, waterless woodland at the corner of Mill Street and Queen for $100.00 an acre in 1872. This land became the newly chartered town's first park, later named Woodside Park. In 1875, five years before his death, Joseph E conveyed the lands to his youngest son Samuel B Schneider who then began to meet demands for building lots in the thriving new town. Before he died in 1912, Samuel made forty-five transfers of land from the original farm including five acres to the Berlin Amateur Athletic Association in the 1880s and 28 acres to the town of Berlin for Victoria Park in 1894. Of all the Schneiders, it was Samuel who undoubtedly witnessed the most radical changes to his physical environment over his

*Taken in the early 20th century, this photograph of the Schneider homestead records the wash house built by Samuel directly behind the main house, the barn in its 'new' location and the path of the creek before it was altered. The large house in the centre background was David Schneider's , the first built on Schneider Avenue (now number 27). Beyond the barn is the 1888 home of Mary and Tobias Schantz, still owned by their descendants, the Russells.*

*The fine Georgian frame farmhouse built by Joseph Schneider is today a living museum. Restored to the mid 1850s, it houses a Schneider 'family' of costumed museum staff who revive for the public the lifestyle of the area's first Pennsylvania-German Mennonite settlers. The family wash house, built in the late 1870s, has been incorporated into the modern museum wing which is connected to the historic house. Exhibits, lectures, workshops, educational programmes and many other activities are presented from mid February to December. Joseph Schneider Haus Museum and Gallery, operated by Region of Waterloo Cultural Services, is home to the nationally acclaimed Canadian Harvest Collection of Germanic folk art.*

lifetime. Indeed, he was an active participant in many of them. He changed the location of the barn, for example, and built a new wash house. Though it still stands today, it no longer bears the same relationship to the creek that the first one did, since even the path of the creek has changed. Before Victoria Park was developed Schneider Creek ran a relatively straight course from Queen to David near Roland rather than cutting diagonally across the Queen Street lots. The creek continues to bear the Schneider name, however, although the road that Joseph built was renamed Queen Street South in the late 1870s.

The last two parts of the farm to be dispersed were on Factory Road and Mill Street. A once prosperous and expansive farm of 448 acres had succumbed to the irrevocable march of progress. David, the brother of the architect of change, remarked wistfully, when interviewed as an old man, "Where once were fields where we worked and raised grain, substantial brick houses and parks have been built." This remains a fitting epitaph to mark the passing of an era.[19]

## "...IT HAS LAND, WATER, WOODS..."

Berlin in the 1890s was an exciting place! Business booming, houses going up, and confidence in the town's future soaring. But one thing did trouble Berliners: the town's limited recreation facilities. The 20 year old Town Park on Queen Street South had been little developed and few citizens ever used it. Waterloo's new park, Westside, officially opened in 1893, was drawing rave reviews. Out-of-town picnic groups flocked there and Berlin's civic pride was stung.

The newspapers of August 1894 focused on the issue with numerous letters, articles and editorials lambasting the lack of picnic facilities, boating, grandstand, fireplaces, benches and

*W V Uttley*

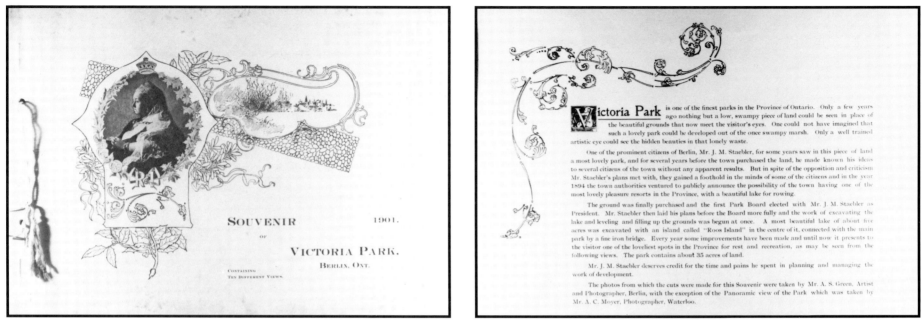

**V**ictoria Park is one of the finest parks in the Province of Ontario. Only a few years ago nothing but a low, swampy piece of land could be seen in place of the beautiful grounds that now meet the visitor's eyes. One could not have imagined that such a lovely park could be developed out of the once swampy marsh. Only a well trained artistic eye could see the hidden beauties in that lonely waste.

One of the prominent citizens of Berlin, Mr. J. M. Staebler, for some years saw in this piece of land a most lovely park, and for several years before the town purchased the land, he made known his ideas to several citizens of the town without any apparent results. But in spite of the opposition and criticism Mr. Staebler's plans met with, they gained a foothold in the minds of some of the citizens and in the year 1894 the town authorities ventured to publicly announce the possibility of the town having one of the most lovely pleasure resorts in the Province, with a beautiful lake for rowing.

The ground was finally purchased and the first Park Board elected with Mr. J. M. Staebler as President. Mr. Staebler then laid his plans before the Board more fully and the work of excavating the lake and leveling and filling up the grounds was begun at once. A most beautiful lake of about five acres was excavated with an island called "Roos Island" in the centre of it, connected with the main park by a fine iron bridge. Every year some improvements have been made and until now it presents to the visitor one of the loveliest spots in the Province for rest and recreation, as may be seen from the following views. The park contains about 35 acres of land.

Mr. J. M. Staebler deserves credit for the time and pains he spent in planning and managing the work of development.

The photos from which the cuts were made for this Souvenir were taken by Mr. A. S. Green, Artist and Photographer, Berlin, with the exception of the Panoramic view of the Park which was taken by Mr. A. C. Moyer, Photographer, Waterloo.

*H S Hallman's 'Souvenir of Victoria Park' caused a minor commotion in 1901. The A S Green photos were fine, the A C Moyer panorama was lovely, but the anonymous introduction raised hackles. There were several obvious errors of fact: the Park Board was never 'elected', did not have a 'President', and J M Staebler had nothing to do with the first Park Board. The real problem however was the complete credit given to Staebler for originating the new park idea. When the booklet appeared, the Park Board issued an official statement to refute those claims. A series of letters in the late July 1901 Berlin News Record enlivened the controversy. Back in 1898, Staebler had resigned from the Park Board chairmanship after accusations from Town Council about misuse of park employees. This may have played a part in the still-simmering bitterness three years later. The Green photos in this 1901 booklet were taken during Victoria Park's opening week in 1896. Moyer's panorama was much more recent.*

other park attractions. The old Town Park was criticized for being too far out of town. Some favoured upgrading the old park but a new idea soon took root.[20]

Someone must have had the first thought of buying the Athletic Club of Berlin's grounds on David Street along with some of Samuel Schneider's wet farmlands. Who this was is lost to history.

W V Uttley quotes William Vogt, strolling along David Street with George DeBus and John Eden as saying "There'd be a fine spot for a central park. It has land, water and woods."[21]

In H S Hallman's *Souvenir of Victoria Park* J M Staebler was given total credit for the new park scheme. This was quickly refuted by an official Park Board communique to the papers as well as a letter from "Fair Play" who claimed William Roos was the real founder.[22] Another claimant to fatherhood could be Daniel Hibner, mayor of Berlin at the time. Also crucially important to the success of the new park development was the Berlin Daily Record. Throughout the mid 1890s its pages continually

*Daniel Hibner*

promoted plans which eventually gave birth to Victoria Park.

In the summer of 1894, 260 ratepayers signed a petition asking that Town Council adopt the province's Public Parks Act and buy the Schneider land and Athletic Club grounds. By provincial law, such a petition compelled council to put the matter to public vote. By-Law 518, as published, mentioned only the Public Parks Act question. But when the electorate approved the measure, many felt their yes-vote also implied approval for the land purchases. The September 28 vote was more than two-to-one in favour and it meant Berlin Town Council now had to appoint six men to a Board of Park Management. The appointees were August Lang, William Roos, L J Breithaupt, J S Hoffman, C F Brown and Thomas Bridger, all well-known names in Berlin business circles. Mayor Hibner was ex officio the seventh member. Berlin's parks (present and future) were now in the hands of an official board working within a budget and relatively free of political interference. The budget was limited to one-half mill on the town's assessment, approximately $1,340.

*H J Bowman*

In the fall of 1894, a long series of meetings, recommendations, arguments and compromises resulted in the Park Board deciding to buy the Athletic Club grounds, about five acres, for $2,500 and 28 acres of Samuel Schneider's farmland and swamp for $3,250. First, town engineer H J Bowman laid out a site plan for the new park. This was upgraded and given more detail by Berlin architect William Hartmuth. But was it feasible; was it practical? An outsider's professional go-ahead could validate the new park, so George Ricker, a well-known landscape engineer from Buffalo was telegraphed and invited to advise the board.

It was a brilliant political stroke. On October 29, 1894 Ricker visited Berlin for less than half a day. His enthusiastic approval was everything the new park supporters could have wished. He suggested keeping the old Town Park for agricultural exhibitions. More importantly, Ricker also favoured acquiring the new lands and putting in a lake with islands and bridges. The two parks could eventually be connected by a "...handsome drive or Boulevard."[23]

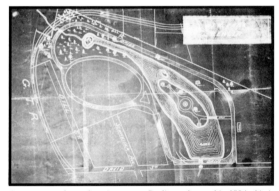

*As arguments for and against a new Berlin park raged in 1894, this is what proponents were trying to sell. Town engineer H J Bowman and architect William Hartmuth worked out an imaginative scheme for Samuel Schneider's farmland and stream. Purchases in later years ensured Dill Street never did slash into the picnic grounds. The original park (and Lot 17) north-western boundary later bulged up to the Preston and Berlin Railway lands when a few acres were bought from neighbouring owners. When George Ricker came to Berlin on October 9 it was this plan he endorsed enthusiastically. Victoria Park's design was home-grown!*

Before completing the purchase, the Park Board first had to agree within itself. Three members wanted to fix up the old Town Park; three were in favour of the new park. While Mayor Hibner was in Chicago on his second honeymoon, the Town Park supporters almost won the day. When Hibner returned, he put his deft political mind to work and on November 24 the board voted to fix up the Town Park and purchase the Athletic Club grounds. Not in the motion, but certainly understood, was that discussions with Samuel Schneider would continue. They did. Within a month, a deal was worked out and the future of the new park was assured.[24]

The original boundaries stretched from David to Heins, southwesterly to the Galt branch of the Grand Trunk Railway tracks, back to the end of Schneider Avenue and along Roland to David. The stream, swamp, meadows, some tillable fields and the landscaped Athletic Club grounds were, as of December 17, 1894, Berlin's new park.

The Bean home at 19 Roland was *"a hive of activity"* in the wintertime. *"There was no place to change your skates in the park,"* recalls Walter Bean, of those days in the late teens and early 1920s, *"all of my friends and all of (his sister) Frances' they all changed in our kitchen. How mother stood it I don't know...she used to keep big tin boxes of biscuits and I think we fed half the army of Kitchener!"*

To buy the land and improve it, plus do some work at the old Town Park, the Park Board asked council to issue a $12,000, 40 year debenture. During 1895 the political bickering and fighting was so heated that at one stage Park Board chairman C F Brown gave council a cheque for $10,000 and said he'd run the park privately! The matter was referred back to the Park Board where no further action was taken.[25] Because there was such strong opposition in town and on council, the debenture didn't go to a public by-law vote until January 6, 1896, when it was approved.

In the meantime, there was work to be done: some fixing-up at the old Town Park was essential. As new owner of the Athletic Club grounds, the Park Board met with various sports groups to prepare schedules for baseball, tennis, cricket, and football (both rugby and soccer).

On April 24, 1895, the Park Board advertised:

Three offers were received. Messrs Shoemaker and Collard of Berlin bid $3,125

**Tenders Wanted.**

TENDERS addressed to the Secretary of the BOARD OF PARK MANAGEMENT will be received up to 7 p.m, on Wednesday the 15th day of May for

**Excavating Artificial Lake and Grading Drives in the New Park, Berlin.**

Plans and specifications may be seen at the Court House and blank forms of tender and any further information may be obtained from H. J. Bowman, Civil engineer.

The lowest or any tender not necessarily accepted.

THOS. BRIDGER,    C. F. BROWN,
Secretary.    Chairman.
Berlin May 4th, 1895.    54-15

*In mid May 1895, William B Hewitt contracted with the Berlin Park Board to excavate the Samuel Schneider farmlands. As work began later that month Hewitt (with front team) and his son Austin (in white shirt) posed with other workers. The main island was built up around the two large elms in the centre. For this first-known view of Berlin's new park, the photographer stood near David Street. Part of the original stream bed meanders at left.*

*One of H A Huber's September 13, 1895 photos shows Swan Island in the centre and part of Roos Island at right. The original grandstand is seen in the right background near the present-day boathouse site. The chimney of the coal-gas plant on Gaukel Street is in centre background. In the foreground, William Hewitt faces the camera, foreman William Collard is in profile to the left and Austin Hewitt is at the plough.*

## AN ISLAND PICNIC

### Inaugural Lunch on the New Park Islet

The much discussed island in the new park is completed and to mark its completion the contractor, Mr W B Hewitt gave a picnic to his employes and a few invited guests on Friday afternoon. The lunch was a very happy affair. At three-thirty in the afternoon, Mr H A Huber went down to the new park and took a view of the upper end of the basin and Swan's island and one of the big island which is yet unchristened. In each instance the brigade of teams and scoops were drawn up in battle array

and had as a background the picturesque island, while dotted here and there as beauty spots were the Chairman of the Park and certain Aldermen and citizens. His work performed, the artist departed and an adjournment was made to a long table, placed near a broad elm on the island, loaded with delicacies, adorned with flowers and presided over by Mrs Hewitt, Mrs Collard and a number of able assistants.

Mr Hewitt and his capable foreman, Mr W. Collard, then seated the picnickers about the board and passed the cider jug. Complimentary references were made to the manner in which the work of excavating had been done and the good health of all concerned drunk in apple-juice. Then with a stiff breeze blowing through their whiskers, Chairman Brown, Reeves Eden and DeBus and Alderman Staebler, Mr Schneider and others lapsed into a deep silence as they vied with each other in doing justice to the ample spread.

The island is about an acre and a half in extent and is beautified by three large, spreading elms and is a very creditable piece of work. Water to the depth of a foot now fills the lower end of the basin and gives one an idea of what the lake will look like when completed. Tenders are now being called for by the Board for the erection of a bridge which will connect the Athletic ground mainland and the island.

If the water hangs out and is sufficient to fill the basin to a depth of four or five feet, and experts think it will be, and with a flotilla of pleasure boats upon the lake, the island nicely planted with trees and shrubs, and the band discoursing sweet music upon it, the new park will be a very popular resort.

It is whispered that the Conservative Nominee for the North Riding will erect a fine band stand on the island for the 29th Batt band. Already a goodly number of those having the leisure time visit the scene and watch the proceedings and well-sinking operations.

As the board was making merry, a wild duck flew about in the air, attracted by the water, and was cheered to the echo and accepted as a good omen.

The thanks of all present were tendered Mr Hewitt and Mr Collard and the ladies

*Downtown Berlin provides backdrop for the second of H A Huber's September 13, 1895 photos. To celebrate the completion of much of the excavation work, Hewitt threw a picnic on the newly-completed island. Huber's view from Roland Street shows the assembled workers and guests before they sat down at the picnic tables arranged by Mrs Hewitt and Mrs Collard.*

and Mr A Farquhar of Toronto $4,490, but the lowest was William B Hewitt of Breslau at $2,850. Told to use only Berlin men and teams, and to complete the job in four months, Hewitt went to work. By mid September he was throwing a picnic on the island to celebrate completion of the excavation.

The new park remained nameless until December 26, 1895 when Park Board By-Law 2, passed December 26, honoured Her Majesty the Queen by naming it "Victoria." The old Town Park was called "Woodside." The large island was named after William Roos and the small adjacent island "Swan." Why the upper island wasn't named isn't known but in 1910 the board corrected the oversight. The seldom-used, but official name, "Schneider Island" honours the original land-owner.

*William B Hewitt (1847-1898) farmer and contractor. In addition to his work in the new park, Hewitt also built Ahrens and Francis Streets in Berlin. Forty years after his death, the Kitchener Daily Record editorial on March 10, 1938 called Victoria Park "his real monument."* [26]

Berlin now had a lake. In winter a lake freezes and in that first Victoria Park winter of 1895-96 an unseen dilemma arose. What would be done with the ice on Victoria Park lake? Should it be cleared and groomed for skating and hockey? Should it be cut and sold for cooling purposes?

In late 1895 the Park Board called for ice-cutting tenders and the best offer was from the Berlin Turf Association. That group had come up with a third possible option: it offered $40 to use the ice surface for horse racing! A second clause in their offer allowed them to cut the ice and sell it for cooling use if the races failed.

Stands were set up on the ice, a course laid out and on February 13, 1896 the first (and only) horse races ever held on Victoria Park lake took place. Within a few weeks, the Turf Association gave up on races and resorted to cutting and selling blocks of ice along the south shore.

However, other Berliners had already staked a claim to the ice. As early as December 7, 1895 scores of youngsters had gathered to enjoy the biggest skating rink any had ever seen. Their enjoyment of the ice wasn't officially approved and, almost predictably, officialdom came out against the frolic. Police Chief Henry Winterhalt warned that any boys caught skating on

Sundays would be prosecuted.

Ice-skating and ice-cutting co-existed warily over the next few decades. The Park Board continued selling the cutting rights but showed little enthusiasm to condition the surface for skating. Nearby residents and dedicated skaters did their own snow-clearing. There was no flooding of the surface until 1914 when the Berlin Fire Department helped out.

By the end of the teens, the Park Board had come to appreciate that skating and hockey were the most valuable winter assets of Victoria Park lake. Clearing, scraping and flooding techniques were developed and soon there was no better outdoor ice in the area. [27]

As well as filling the lake, water was needed in the park to quench visitors' thirsts. In fall 1895

The first day's sport at Victoria park was very good considering the inclement weather and a consequently heavy track. The attendance was fair.

The result of the two events was as follows :—

2. 50 TROT OR PACE, PURSE $1.25.

| | | | | | | |
|---|---|---|---|---|---|---|
| King Billy, J Murphy | 1 | 3 | 5 | 1 | 2 | 1 |
| Hazel G, A Brown | 4 | 1 | 1 | 3 | 4 | 2 |
| Little Flo, P Fillman | 5 | 5 | 4 | 4 | 1 | 3 |
| Tom Appleby, R Porter | 3 | 4 | 2 | 2 | 3 | 0 |
| Little Dan, C Reinhardt | | | | | | |
| Little Casino, S Cook | | | | | | |
| Texas Minnie, C R Pollakowski | | | | | | |

Time :—2.23; 2.22; 2.25; 2.23; 2.23;

Augusta Kruse was 84 years old in 1949 when she sat down for what must be one of Kitchener's earliest tape-recorded oral histories. Through most of her life she had lived in the Victoria Park vicinity and clearly recalled the mid 1890s. *"There was no street between Queen and David... (where Courtland now is)... that was an orchard. There was just Schneider's farm and just a creek ran through. They took out all the sand to make a lake, by horses and by hand."* Following that busy summer of 1895 Augusta thinks of the park's first winter when *"...all the people that had skates came and there were so many the first Christmas and New Year's that they could hardly get around."*

*In the winter of 1897 or 1898, Joseph M Snyder (left ,in hat, nephew of Samuel Schneider) met friend Ed Detweiler and they smile for the camera. Young and old have already taken to Victoria Park's ice in this, the earliest known skating photo.*

well-drillers were at work and the newspapers charted their course daily. Finally on September 30 at 172 feet a fine flowing well was declared.

*Reuben Bowman's 1896 boathouse provided year-round service, once the Park Board accepted that skating was an activity worth supporting. In this photo from the 1920s is seen a special wooden entrance shelter.*

However the clear and abundant water was sulphurous. The drillers went back to work but hit solid rock at 200 feet. The sulphur water was seen as an asset by Berliners and soon a trip to Victoria Park wasn't complete without a sip of the mineral refreshment. A visiting American even declared that if the flow was strong enough he'd form a syndicate and build a mammoth health resort. The spa never did develop but until the 1920s a pump and hanging tin cups marked a special spot in the park. When the new Japanese-style pergola was installed nearby in 1921, its sanitary drinking fountains were hooked up to city water mains. The first well remains, hidden, burrowing 200 feet into the blue clay and bedrock underlying Kitchener.

*In the September 12, 1896 Record, Messrs A S Green and Co, Photographers, announced for sale a series of ten Victoria Park views at 50¢ each. Taken within days of the park's official opening they provide a stunning catalogue of its original vistas.*

*Another of A S Green's late summer 1896 park portraits provides an interesting contrast with a similar view taken by H A Huber a year earlier. The main bridge is now in place and the bandstand is ready for music. The grandstand remains in its original site but will be moved to the foot of Richmond Avenue in April 1897.*

Early 1896 saw many Victoria Park projects underway.

On the main bridge to Roos Island one can still see the manufacturer's medallion: "Central Bridge Engineering Co Lim Peterboro Ont...Erected 1896." Built in early May the bridge has stood the test of time, although in 1974-75 it underwent a complete refurbishing at a cost of $25,300. The original 1896 cost? $740!

Reuben Bowman, a well-known Berlin carpenter, was busy on the David Street shore. In little over a month, his 70 foot $327 boathouse was in use. It lasted until 1930.

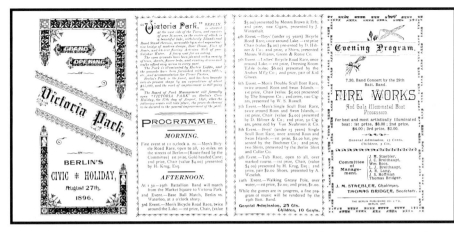

Rest and relaxation in Victoria Park quickly became part of many Berliners' Sunday afternoons. On a neatly clipped Roos Island (ca 1897-99) this quartet risks censure for straying from the pathways. Caretaker Fritz Kruse and his occasional help had quickly put the park's lawns, gardens and shrubs in good order.

The park's next adornment was a gem! The athletic grounds' grandstand area had already hosted park music concerts but a real bandstand was needed. As George Ricker had suggested, the island was an ideal location. Within 30 days, public donations had paid for a 25 foot octagonal structure in the centre of Roos Island. Thursday evening, August 13,1896 Berlin's Band of the 29th Regiment inaugurated the new bandstand, but "to prevent the grass and beds on the island being trodden down, the people were not permitted to cross the Venetian bridge, three special constables barring ingress."[28]

Early photos show a wooden fence around Victoria Park and gates at the David and Water entrances. These were installed to control and charge admission fees on occasions when sporting or musical events were scheduled. Because of the physical layout of Victoria Park and its athletic grounds, it was not possible to separate the two areas. Anyone in the park proper could easily walk over to the grandstand or bandstand and enjoy the performance free. Only at the entrance gates could admission be charged. This arrangement caused many arguments, both physical and legal, right from the earliest days. The issue wasn't cleared up until 1908 when a long canvas fence enclosed the open side of the athletic grounds and separate admission could be controlled. Then the wooden fences around Victoria Park were removed. The frustration of the Berliner can be sensed from the Daily Record's columnist, "The Man on the Bell Tower" on August 14, 1896.

"Here we pay a band to play every Thursday evening for the public (downtown) on Market Square and we're taxed for this. We bought the park and we're taxed to pay for it: we go down and are charged to get in. It's just a little too much...!"

The same four young people shown above are enjoying another of Victoria Park's attractions. The previously healthy elm trees are now gaunt and dying. Other elms farther from the lake survived, and more were planted, but in the 1960s Dutch Elm disease wiped out most of these stately trees.

The Victoria Park scene is set...set for the Grand Opening and the town is ready to celebrate!

## Official Opening: Victoria Park
### Berlin, Ontario
### July 1, 1896
### In Attendance, His Excellency
### Lord Aberdeen, Governor-General of Canada
### and Her Excellency, Lady Aberdeen

That was the original plan, according to the May 28 Park Board meeting but the Governor-General's schedule prevented his attending. Those first ceremonies were scrapped and the next thing Berliners heard about a Grand Opening was in mid July when a new date, August 27, was announced.

On August 15, the newspapers published a full list of the day's events. Their article was basically a reprint of the large, red, white and blue poster which soon appeared all over Berlin. Two hundred were printed but only one is known to exist today. Its presence in the archives is complemented by a rough, pencilled draft on the letterhead of 'Randall and Roos, Wholesale Grocers' undoubtedly penned by Park Board member William Roos.[29]

In addition to the advertised activities, many other attractions entertained the crowds. Kids enjoyed J Wallace's merry-go-round which cost him a $10 fee to the Park Board. William Tyler's 'throwing-balls-at-dolls' game caught the fancy of some. In the evening J Landreth's decorative coloured lights strung on the bridge and in trees earned him $10.

Rain threatened early in the day but all turned out well for Berlin's big celebration. A L Anderson's review in the next day's Daily Telegraph gives not only the details but a good overall flavour of what a holiday was like in late 19th century Berlin.

For visitors who hadn't previously been to the park, it must have been an eye-opener! Fifteen months earlier the area was poor farmland, a small stream, straggly scrub bush and cedar swamp. The vision of the early 1890s park enthusiasts had been carried out.[30]

## BERLIN'S CIVIC HOLIDAY.

### GRAND OPENING OF VICTORIA PARK.

#### A Season of Self-Congratulation, Rejoicing and Amusement.

In the great majority of inland towns in Canada, the Civic Holiday is being made the occasion of an exodus, preferably to some river or lake side, but anywhere to get rid, for the time being, of one's dry and monotonous surroundings. Nor can any reasonable objection be urged where, as it so frequently happens, the conditions necessary to an enjoyable outing, are but sparsely supplied at home. In the latter respect kind Nature has, fortunately for Berlin, been in no wise niggardly of her endowments, and the result is (with the skillfully applied aid of art) one of unquestionably the finest home Parks to be found anywhere in Canada. But we must not at present elaborate.

The morning opened auspiciously, but when about 8 o'clock it commenced to get cloudy the expressions of regret were as loud and general as though the crowning issue of life were at stake. A couple of hours later, however, the sun made its appearance and with it came crowds of smiling people of both sexes, invariably arrayed in their best and evidently intent on having a day's sport and enjoyment. And they had their wish, as Berlinites always have, seeing that everything they undertake they never fail to accomplish—particularly the ladies, who yesterday appear to have turned out en masse. The only thing that momentarily marred the harmony of the morning's enjoyment was a little friction between the baseball team and the Board of Park Management, but the difficulty was soon adjusted.

The first event and the only one on the programme for the forenoon was the Men's Bicycle Road Race, which took place about 11 o'clock and was witnessed by hundreds of interested spectators. After dinner and promptly at 1.30 o'clock the fine Band of the 29th Batt. appeared on the Market Square (their uniforms and instruments all in first-class holiday trim) and having formed in marching order, struck up a stirring march, to the sweet strains of which the crowd wended their way along King to Foundry street, up Foundry to John, thence to David and along David street to Victoria Park, where the amusements of the day commenced. The large number of people who witnessed the base ball game played between the Berlin and Waterloo clubs indicated that the proceeds of the gate must have been quite large.

Another very laughable feature of the occasion was the attempt to walk the greased pole with the invariable accompaniment of a head-first souce into the all too receptive water.

The scull races were largely patronized and passed off without friction save that in the men's double scull race F. Fricker and James Duck's boat was fouled, and claim that the race should have been rowed over. Doubtless every justice will be shown in the case. This ended the sports for the day, the Band all the time discoursing their sweetest selections.

The Park in the evening, with its meandering walks, fragrant flower plots and other charming scenic features, ablaze in electric illumination, and dotted at short intervals throughout the length and breadth of its water area with canoes, skiffs and other craft; the crowds of visitors, young and old, perambulating the grounds or from the banks or bridge looking on while listening to the enchanting music; the fireworks, etc.—all these taken together constituted the numbers of an evening programme rarely excelled and which will years hence be recalled as one of the most enjoyable ever held in Berlin.

# "...HARD TO FIND ANOTHER MAN..."

Frederick 'Fritz' Kruse was named Victoria Park's first caretaker on March 19, 1896. Working full-time eight months a year, and four months as-needed, he earned $250, increased to $540 by the time he died. A native of Mecklenburg, Germany, Kruse came to Canada in 1868 at age 28.

From the time of his hiring, Victoria Park became his second home. All the initial planting of the park was under his hand: shrubs, flowerbeds, lawns, terraces, trees. His devotion and long hours — supplemented by some summer help — made Victoria Park a growing place of beauty. Some of the park's oldest trees, Norway Spruce and Silver Maple near the pavilion, date from the Kruse era. Apart from horticultural duties, Kruse looked after the park's growing animal and bird collection. He was also a de facto constable and many youths faced his wrath when caught vandalising or using profanity. In 1904 he had to carry a gun to destroy dogs that were harassing the park's deer herd.

Among Karl Mueller's remembrances as Park Board chairman were some fond ones of Fritz. Each Sunday, Kruse would report to Mueller, usually with a litany of complaints about mischief done by boys. Mueller concludes "...he would have liked it best if the park had been there for him and the chairman alone...."[31]

At his death, July 15, 1913, a Park Board member said: "...in these days when everyone wants to do as little as he can for the highest wages...it will be hard to find another man like Fritz." Kruse was the first of three men who would leave their marks on Victoria Park in the caretaker/superintendent position.

*Like clockwork, each Sunday morning, Fritz Kruse would give his weekly park report to chairman Karl Mueller. Mueller built this home at 23 Roland in 1897 and it is currently designated under the Ontario Heritage Act.*

# "...WHEN THEY ARE REQUIRED..."

What's the oldest man-made object in Victoria Park? If the serial number is any indicator, the cannon in front of the Queen Victoria monument wins. It and its twin on Roos Island have been in the park since November 1895. That's when the Park Board signed a bond agreement with Canada's Minister of Militia and Defence for the loan of two "...24 pr., 50 cwt. guns from Militia Stores in the City of Kingston...(and they)... shall be properly cared for and returned into the Militia stores...when they are required...."[32]

The Grand Trunk Railroad delivered the guns free but not until May 1898 did the Park Board hire George Schlee and pay him $48 to mount them. According to photographic evidence the two cannon have been in the original sites ever since, although the concrete mounts have been changed.

These are the Victoria Park guns most people recognize, but there were others.

In the afterglow of World War I, communities all across Canada requested captured German field-pieces for their parks and cemeteries. In January 1919, the Kitchener Park Board asked MP W D Euler for a pair of cannon "...the more battle-scarred the better...."[33] On their June arrival the two guns were placed at the Courtland entrance and they were even used in a

*Two captured German field-pieces were presented to the Park Board in 1919. Two years later they were mounted in concrete facing west in the playground area. This enlarged portion of a mid 1920s photo by Dorothy Russell is the best available shot of these guns.*

*Matt Potje Jr, son of Victoria Park's head gardener, isn't really sure he wants to be quite so high off the ground, in this August 1930 photo with his godmother Mrs Margaret Marx. The original 1898 cannon mount has deteriorated badly. In the background is one of the park's newer flagpoles, whose concrete base is still in place in 1996.*

1920 Musical Tattoo and Carnival in the athletic park. Soon afterwards the guns were set in concrete in the playground, west of the pavilion site.

During World War II, the scrap-metal drive claimed these trophies. As Kitchener's colourful mayor, Joe Meinzinger put it: "...I think it would be poetic justice to have these captured cannon...found sufficiently useful to help blast the Nazis from the face of the earth...."[34]

Every once in a while someone agitates for the removal of the two old cannon from the park. In fact, one of the Park Board's longest-serving members, Oscar Lauber, lobbied unsuccessfully against them in the 1950s.[35]

Generations of Berlin/Kitchener kids have made beelines to the guns when they visit Victoria Park. Whatever they were in the past, in the eyes of children, they are interactive sculptures.

# "...FIRST, LAST & ALWAYS, CANADIANS..."

In Berlin/Kitchener's history, there is probably no topic more asked-about than the Kaiser's bust. And probably no topic more misunderstood.

The history of the bust is rooted in the Franco-Prussian War. Prussia led a coalition of many German states, defeating France and creating the

*Seen close up and angled properly, the Kaiser's bust etches a strong figure against the Berlin sky. Homes at 29 and 33 Roland Street provide background. This photo of ca 1903 shows the concrete base suffering some deterioration.*

*Following his tour of the town and Victoria Park, Prince Louis of Battenberg lifted his hat to the photographer on the steps of the pavilion. Some Berliners were disappointed that he did not wear military uniform, but the prince had specifically requested an unceremonious visit. Moments after this August 30, 1905 snapshot, he addressed the 1,200 people present in German. He thanked the town for its hospitality and praised the evident prosperity. The Band of the 29th Regiment entertained and the Prince told Mayor Kranz had never heard any better.*

German Empire. With victory in 1871, Wilhelm I of Prussia became emperor (Kaiser) of Germany and a hero to Germans around the world.

In Berlin, Ontario, the peace, Kaiser Wilhelm I and the new empire were celebrated joyously with a *Friedensfest* — a festival of peace, of freedom. Parades, concerts, choirs, speeches, along with good food and drink attracted upwards of 10,000 people from across Ontario, many of German background. It was the newly-proclaimed town's biggest event. To symbolize the hopes of that period a 'Deutsche Eiche' (German oak) was planted in front of the Court House.

The Berlin Concordia Society held a 25-year commemoration of the 1871 Friedensfest in May 1896. It was noted that the Deutsche Eiche had died so a new one was to be planted. By September that idea grew into a public subscription for a Peace Memorial in honour of the original Friedensfest. It was to

*A 1905 postcard view crowds five early Victoria Park objects into one small scene. The pavilion, mounted cannon and bandstand decorate the background while an early-style bench is seen at right. The Peace Memorial with Kaiser's bust and medallion of Bismarck is nicely outlined from close-up.*

*The name Louis J Breithaupt resonates through the history of late 19th century Berlin. His tenure on the Park Board from 1894 to 1909 interests us. As detailed in his personal diaries, August 13, 1897 was important not only for Victoria Park but for L J personally.[39]*

be a granite monument topped by a larger-than-life bust of the now-dead Kaiser Wilhelm I. The News Record supported the fund while the Telegraph fumed "...our town will enjoy the doubtful distinction of being the only place in the British Empire where the statue of a foreign monarch is erected in a public resort."[36]

Donations came quickly. Many German-background people contributed but the list also contained names such as McFarlane, Eden, Cosgrove, Clemens and Peterson. Waterloo North MP Joseph Seagram added $50.[37] The order was sent to Martin and Pilzing Company of Berlin, Germany for a bust "...of copper, made by artificers by hand...after the model of the celebrated sculptor Reinhold Begas."[38]

It stood four feet high, weighed 150 pounds and cost $250. Also ordered were two bronze medallions honouring Otto von Bismarck, Wilhelm's foreign minister, and Helmuth von Moltke, the army chief of staff in 1871. The medallions were to be attached to the monument and were gifts of George Sleeman of Guelph and Dr Lentze, the German consul in Montreal. The base and die for the monument arrived in late June 1897. Both were of polished Quebec granite and together weighed 12 tons.

A year earlier the Friedensfest Peace Memorial Committee had requested a site in Victoria Park. It was agreed the Kaiser would look northwards over the athletic grounds from a point on the lakeshore near the much later Japanese pergola. With the monument up and the bust and medallions installed, the official unveiling ceremony was set for Friday, August 13, 1897.

Foreshadowing the dramatic and turbulent future of the bust, both Dr Lentze and Park Board chairman J M Staebler, who were to have officiated at the unveiling, were injured in separate accidents just days before the event. Staebler had been helping to erect the park's new 'German' flagpole when it slipped and drove him to the ground.

Special trains were scheduled to bring many out-of-town German societies to Berlin for the historic occasion. Bands and singers paraded to the park where hundreds of people had gathered. There, by the lake, was the shrouded Peace Memorial.

The Concordia Society's John Motz and Toronto-based German Consul A S Nordhimer addressed the crowd. Both stressed the memorial in no way compromised the loyalty all Germans in Canada felt to the Queen. Nordhimer, utilizing the latest technology, pressed an electric button. The drapery fell, and hearty outbursts of cheering and 'hochs' followed.

Mayor J C Breithaupt of Berlin accepted the monument for the town. "We

*Victoria Park.*
*Aug. 1. 1914.*

*Arguably Berlin/Kitchener's most famous photograph, this August 23, 1914 Ernest Denton shot was, until recently, a group of anonymous people. Research for this book identified, from left, R E Bush, the park boat-keeper; Otto Knechtel; Gordon Maier; unknown, Clayton Maier. In the third boat, behind the bust, is Carl Knechtel. The face in the crook of Otto's right arm is unidentified, as is the partial figure at left standing on the David Street boathouse dock. Between Otto and Gordon note the gasoline engine in the second boat. In 1915, Bush was ordered to remove this powered launch from the lake.[41]*

*Among the photographs taken by her grandfather, W G Cleghorn, Margaret Farrow discovered this faded and flawed, but historically fascinating, version of the famous bust-in-the-boat shot. Only two boats are tied up to the boathouse dock. The third can be seen behind Gordon Maier. One might presume the third boat is still heading towards the dock, thus this more relaxed group shot was taken moments before the famous photograph. The two Knechtel boys were sons of Charles Knechtel, the architect of Victoria Park's original pavilion, comfort station and present boathouse.*

are proud of our German descent but we are first, last and always, Canadians." Turning to his brother Louis J Breithaupt of the Park Board, he presented the Peace Memorial to the board. Speaking in both English and German, L J hoped the Peace Memorial would be an "...incentive to our children and grandchildren to deeds both good and great...." He also pointed out that the present German emperor, Wilhelm II, was grandson to the just-unveiled Wilhelm I and to the park's namesake, Queen Victoria.[40]

More music, dancing, a picnic and games made this an exciting day in Berlin, Ontario. Exciting, but portentous! Another attraction in Victoria Park, but a seed had been sown....

❦

*Events in Berlin during 1915-16 captured headlines around the country. An issue of the Toronto Star in March 1916 carried this photo which had been taken on February 16. That's when members of the 118th Battalion pried the two medallions from the Peace Memorial and held them proudly for the camera. The large house in left background is 101 David, the Quickfall home.*

In September of that year, 30 ex-soldiers who had served under Wilhelm I held a reunion in Berlin and placed wreaths on the Peace Memorial. Senator Samuel Merner, a veteran himself, reminisced about the earlier Kaiser's good qualities. Prince Louis of Battenberg, a German aristocrat who had married a granddaughter of Queen Victoria and was now an admiral in the British navy, visited Berlin in August 1905. As the carriage carrying Prince Louis and Mayor Carl Kranz passed the Kaiser's bust, Battenberg doffed his hat but made no comment. Back in Germany, the Battenbergs and the Kaiser's family were not the closest of friends.[42]

*On a sunny afternoon in 1915, dressed in their Sunday best, two young men find time for some high-jinx on the Peace Memorial. This grainy snapshot is the only known rear view of the monument.*

❦

Most Berliners saw the Peace Memorial as an attractive addition to the park. They'd look at it, take a picture, read the inscriptions, perhaps sit on the stepped pedestal and put on their skates. It blended in well with the park and from 1911 on shared honours with the larger Queen Victoria sculpture.

**1914.** The story of Berlin during World War I has been told in many forms. The Kaiser's bust figures into the story both literally and symbolically.

Having a bust of the grandfather of the enemy's leader in the park became a sore point with some members of the community. Late on Saturday night, August 22, 1914, three young Berlin men, Fred Bolton, Alan Smith and John Ferguson pulled it down, hauled it to the Roos Island bridge and

*Between the theft of the medallions on February 16 and the monument's removal on March 1, the granite cap was toppled and graffiti painted on the die. The two flags waving atop the monument are possibly those being displayed by the soldiers in the previous photograph. Skaters found the granite steps handy for changing footgear.*

*Seen from the west, the Peace Memorial provides a good view of the medallion honouring Helmuth von Moltke. The scalloped form of the Kaiser's bust is revealed.*

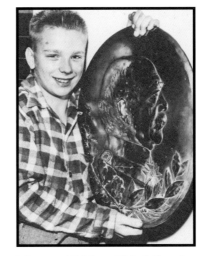

*Forty years after it disappeared, the medallion of Otto von Bismarck suddenly re-appeared in Toronto. Floyd Migory holds the battered bronze portrait which his father had purchased from an ex-Berlin resident. The medallion re-surfaced in 1996 along with a second known napkin ring said to be made from the melted-down Kaiser's bust.*

toppled it into the lake. When the bust was noticed missing Sunday morning, the lake near the pedestal was dragged. W J Near of 39 Roland Street said that about 2 o'clock he'd heard a splash and saw three men running away. Acting on this information, searchers moved to the bridge where Police Constable Meehan and the park's boat-keeper R E Bush spotted the bust. Some neighbourhood youngsters dove in, attached a rope and helped drag the muddy Kaiser to shore. Later, those boys, the bust and Bush posed for what has become Berlin's most famous photograph.

Meanwhile those three men left town on Sunday. When they returned on Wednesday, police arrested the trio. Later reports describe the three as soldiers or militia members but, as with much of the story around the toppling of the Kaiser's bust, contemporary evidence is vague. Charged under Park By-Law 7, all three pled guilty under representation by D S Bowlby. Several adjournments were granted but there was no final outcome in court.

Bolton and Smith are listed in the August 29, 1914 Berlin Daily Telegraph as joining the Canadian Army's First Contingent at Valcartier, Quebec. On September 17, Bolton was back home, suffering from an attack of appendicitis. Curiously, both the Record and Telegraph printed nearly-identical complimentary articles, neither mentioning the bust incident. By January, Bolton is on the lists of the Canadian Mounted Rifles, Third Contingent, in London, Ontario. Ferguson's military career in the early days of the war isn't as clear but note the Daily Telegraph's headline of November 17, 1917: *'Man Who Pulled Down Kaiser's Bust Is Killed'*. The brief item mentions Ferguson enlisting in Guelph and being fatally wounded on October 30 in France.

The bust itself wasn't badly damaged and was repaired for $17.25. Recognising the potential for a repeat of the incident, the Park Board agreed to the Concordia Society's request to store it in their club rooms for the war's duration.

The Kaiser's bust next appears on February 15, 1916 when a mob of civilians and soldiers ransacked the Concordia's premises and hauled the statue onto King Street. Abuse was hurled at the bust: sticks, canes, boots, spittle and worse represented the mob's feeling. Dragged up and down King Street, then lugged along Queen South to the lock-up at the soldiers' barracks, the Kaiser had made his last public journey.

Looking back at that night in Berlin history, it is tempting to point the finger of blame. In those days of 1915-16, Berlin was an embattled place. The recruiting techniques of the local battalion (the 118th), the name-change controversy and racial hatreds combined to put the city in the spotlight. On a grander scale, the nation, along with Berlin, was undergoing the worst war anyone had ever known. Technology, heretofore seen as a great blessing, was making death possible on a previously undreamt-of scale. All communications systems were strictly controlled. Information about the war and the enemy was totally one-sided.

The Kaiser, torn from his Victoria Park pedestal and missing ever since, remains symbolic of a time in our city's history which must not be forgotten.[43]

The bust itself is certainly not forgotten. Rumours about its fate grew over the years. The most common of these had the bust taken to the 118th's training camp at Carling Heights near London. There it was melted down and made into napkin rings featuring a crest of the 118th. This story begins in the September 20, 1956 issue of the Kitchener-Waterloo Record. An uncredited story quoting an anonymous woman is the first published reference to the souvenir napkin rings. Photos of a napkin ring and the plaque of Bismarck lend credence to the story. Both the medallion and that napkin ring are now in a Toronto collector's possession.

Ten years later, October 4, 1966, Record writer Jim Widdecombe interviewed an anonymous ex-member of the 118th Battalion. Presenting one of the souvenir napkin rings to Doon Pioneer Village, this man also claimed to be a shadowy fourth man involved in the toppling of the bust. Although his story is flawed historically, it does give another twist to the tale. This napkin ring, still in the (now renamed) Doon Heritage Crossroads collection, is the only publicly accessible item purported to be made from the melted-down 150 lb bust.

From two anonymous sources in these two Kitchener-Waterloo Record articles of 40 and 30 years ago, springs the melted-down theory of what happened to the Kaiser's bust. [44]

An early ceremony around the Queen Victoria monument. Judging by the size of the nearby trees, this is probably a pre WWI snapshot, but the exact event is not known. Gordon Eby took this and many other photographs of the community's activities. In the background are houses on Water Street South and Frank's Lane.[45]

# "...IN EVERY SENSE A NATIONAL POSSESSION..."
*Marion Heath*

Queen Victoria's Diamond Jubilee, celebrating her 60 years on the throne, was approaching. Patriotic devotion combined with an almost cult-like adoration of Victoria was fervent throughout her far-flung empire. Her subjects in Berlin were no exception.

Thus, in 1895, as Berlin's new park approached completion, its naming became part of this adoration and the choice was inevitable. Victoria Park it would be. This beautiful new park would personify the dignity, grace and charm of the queen and empress.

In 1896 the press called for public subscriptions to put up a statue of Queen Victoria. Visitors to the park often asked why there was nothing to honour its namesake; nothing to complement the bust of her daughter's father-in-law, Kaiser Wilhelm I.

*Casper Braun*

Victoria's death in January 1901 prompted patriotic meetings aimed at raising $5,000. Local MP Joseph Seagram pledged $500 but when Berlin Town Council opted for a Memorial Hall instead, the statue fund stalled.

The Princess of Wales Chapter of the Imperial Order of the Daughters of the Empire was organized in 1903 with Mrs Joseph Seagram as one of its vice-presidents. The March 14 initial meeting passed a motion to "...get a statue of our late beloved Sovereign, Queen Victoria, to be placed in Victoria Park...."[46]

It took five years, scores of money-raising events such as concerts, dances, musicals, operas, bake-and-handwork sales and even a racehorse auction to raise sufficient funds to call for tenders in 1908.

Cavaliere Raffaele Zaccaquini of Rome, Italy was already well-known in Berlin. His statue of Rev Dr Louis Funcken at St Jerome's College attracted admiration and he was commissioned to sculpt the Queen's figure. Father Weiler, a Berlin Resurrectionist stationed in Rome, paid regular visits to Zaccaquini's studio. Tourists, such as Mr and Mrs S J Williams in March 1909, wrote back describing it "...ready to be fused in bronze...."[47] Rome's leading daily Corrierre d'Italia, commended the "...truly sovereign pose and perfect resemblance of the work...."[48]

Meanwhile, back in Berlin, Braun's Marble Works completed the pedestal by late 1909, Casper Braun declaring that even an earthquake could not destroy it. The base was 36 slabs of Stanstead granite from Quebec cemented together and placed on a cement foundation. The die was a solid cube of granite four feet square weighing eight tons and was cemented in place on the base with lead.

Like the monument rising over the Victoria Park skyline, costs too began to rise. The statue itself cost $2,800, freight $427.50, the pedestal was $2,450 and though the lion was free it incurred $97 in freight charges. Incidental costs brought the IODE's overall total to $5,895.40. With the intervention of MP William Lyon Mackenzie King in Ottawa, no import duties were levied.

Berliners were getting impatient about their statue, but at long last on October 20, 1910 it arrived at the Grand Trunk Railway station. The lion and royal banner had arrived in July so finally all the pieces were together. Under Braun's careful eye the ten foot statue was soon positioned atop the 18 foot pedestal and Victoria soared into the park sky.

The death of King Edward VII that year cancelled all vice-regal engagements so the Governor-General was unable to attend an unveiling. Through the long winter of 1910, the Queen's statue stood, draped in canvas.

Spring! The big day: Monday, May 29, 1911. Governor-General Earl Grey, his two daughters and his party pulled into the Berlin train station. Mayor W H Schmalz, civic dignitaries, 200 Boy Scouts, the Grey's Horse guard of honour and the Band of the 29th Regiment provided escort for his carriage. Thousands of enthusiastic citizens, enjoying their half-holiday, lined the route from station to Town Hall to Victoria Park.

*From all angles, Zaccaquini's statue radiates majesty in Victoria Park. William Roos led a 1912 campaign to put iron railings around the monument. The 1920s view shows it didn't always keep people out. By the 1930s the railing was gone but an attractive concrete vase and colourful flowerbeds lent beauty to the site. Note the tennis net posts at right.*

25

*Young and old have never been able to resist climbing onto the lion for a snapshot. This 1930s view was found in an antique shop in 1996 and nothing is known of the subjects perched on the monument. In the background can be seen the Victoria Park greenhouses.*

As the dignitaries took their places on the platform erected near the draped statue, an estimated ten thousand people gathered around. Five hundred children, in the nearby Richmond Avenue grandstand, sang 'Rule Britannia' after which IODE Princess of Wales Chapter regent, Mrs Mahlon Davis addressed His Excellency, reaffirming Berlin's love and loyalty to King and country. The Governor-General responded, the choir sang, a prayer was said, and then Earl Grey pulled the rope to unveil Her Majesty's statue.

A momentary stillness.

All eyes were riveted on the enormous Union Jack slowly dropping from Victoria's crown to the ground. Her gradual unveiling and the statue's splendour caused the crowd to erupt into an ovation so loud the band's National Anthem could barely be heard.

Earl Grey noted how Berlin always endeavoured to do things better than anyone else. He said he had been unprepared for the exceptional beauty of this statue. "It is fitting that Berlin, the City of happy homes, should be crowned with a statue of Victoria the Good, the presiding genius and guardian angel of the home...."

In his speech he also referred to the previous week's unveiling of the National Memorial of Queen Victoria in front of Buckingham Palace.

William Lyon Mackenzie King, MP, a son of Berlin, called this a memorable achievement on three levels — municipal, national, international. It brought great recognition to Berlin which was to become a city soon. Likewise the IODE displayed hard work and loyal devotion in obtaining the statue which had now been added to the few historic monuments in Canada. "...because of the conception and artistic quality... (it is) ... in every sense a national possession...."[49]

Internationally, he too paralleled the Berlin unveiling by people of German and English descent to that of the memorial in London a week earlier. There, two grandsons of the Queen had presided: one the German, Kaiser Wilhelm II; the other soon to become King George V.

Her travelling days over, Queen Victoria towered regally over the young trees in the park. That first evening, she witnessed the season's opening concert by the Band of the 29th Regiment.

❧

Until the 1940s, Victoria's monument was a rallying place for Empire and Victoria Day celebrations. IODE ladies held a 'Decoration of Queen Victoria Monument' ceremony by unfurling the Union Jack and blanketing the lion with flowered wreaths. The mayor, aldermen, veterans, school children and citizens attended while the band accompanied choirs singing patriotic songs.

Gradually, fewer and fewer people attended Empire Day ceremonies. Formal school programs gave way to track-and-field exercises in the nearby athletic grounds. By the mid 1960s, when the grandstand was torn down, schools no longer marched to Victoria Park in May. Still, the IODE kept faith by placing wreaths in tribute.

Ultimately, as the sun set on the fabled British Empire, even these celebrations faded away. For several years, on Victoria Day, the statue stood alone but still grand. In the 1990s a small celebration was started again and the faintest of smiles can be seen on Victoria's face.

❧

The Victorian era awakened interest in science and exploration, elaborate and attractive home furnishings and the improvement of minds. Victoria's own virtues are stated with admirable Victorian sentiment (and brevity) in the inscription on the die:

Victoria, Queen, Empress,
A Model Wife and Mother.
Beloved, Admired, Revered,
She Shall Live In The
Hearts of Her People.

(And in her park in Kitchener, Ontario, Canada.)

# "...A TWENTIETH CENTURY PARK..."

In the two decades between the Grand Opening and the First World War, visitors flocked to Victoria Park. A clamour soon arose for more improvements, more attractions, more facilities. Restricted to the half-mill on Berlin's assessment, the Park Board could only carry out a few of the many suggestions. Six major park features were initiated in the 1896-1914 period: the original pavilion, the comfort station, the deer run and animal pens, roadways, bridges and athletic grounds renovations.

## Pavilion:

Calls for a pavilion began within a year of the Grand Opening. There was no resting place for visitors and if it rained, picnickers had no shelter. The

*A good close up of the original Victoria Park pavilion in 1907. On the second-floor balcony, Frank and Worth Schantz gaze out over the park. Some of the building's shutters are still in place. During fine weather the entire main floor and upper turrets were opened wide to the elements. At right is the kitchen and picnic shelter portion while the two turrets anchor the pavilion's north end.*

News Record on June 12, 1897 demanded the Park Board "...do something to seat the public and a pavilion is the solution."

Architect Charles Knechtel developed some rough plans in 1900 but lack of money delayed action. Subsequently the High Park pavilion in Toronto caught a Park Board committee's eye so Knechtel's design was modified. An $8,000 debenture issue in August 1901 provided $5,000 for pavilion use and tenders were called that fall. The old Saengerfest Hall/exhibition building at Woodside Park was being torn down at the time and the board demanded bidders reduce their fees by using as much lumber as possible

*An early view of the pavilion with a balloon ascension demonstration and tents set up. This photo was probably taken around 1902-05 and shows the south end of the pavilion with the kitchen area at left.*

from that structure. Work began in April 1902, the foundations were done by May, the roof was on by June's end and the official opening held August 15th.

The Band of the 29th Regiment entertained and George 'Pop' Philip's fireworks, especially the naval battle scene, were a big hit. Twenty-two hundred people attended the evening's event and many stayed for an impromptu dance afterwards. That dance was the first of thousands to be held in the park's two pavilions, but dancing created controversy in the early part of this century. By 1914, neighbours were complaining of the

*From many angles the Victoria Park pavilion presented dramatic vistas. Approaching from the east, a park visitor received the full width of the building with two soaring turrets and an even taller lantern crowning the roof. Noting the comfort station's site allows one to position the pavilion perfectly. Already reaching twenty feet in height in 1911, the evergreens at right are now, 85 years later, among the park's oldest and tallest trees.*

noise while the Berlin and Waterloo Ministerial Association petitioned the board to eliminate dancing, which "...tended to lower the morals."[50] At least two Park Board members agreed, but in the end dances were recognized as revenue producers and they continued.

Refreshment sales in the pavilion were another source of revenue for the Park Board. Fred Gregor was the best known of the old pavilion's restaurateurs and his tables were favourite rendezvous for young and old.

Gordon Eby was a direct descendant of Berlin founder Bishop Benjamin Eby. His diaries for this period provide several glimpses of Victoria Park. SUNDAY, JULY 14, 1912: (Gordon has just been boating with his friend, Della) *"We went over to the pavillion, had some ice cream, then had a pleasant walk home. It was a fine evening."* A FORTNIGHT LATER: *"...wheeled up to the park, wheeled around a little, had some ice cream at the pavillion, at the same table where two weeks before...Della...had sat. Well, I went home."*[51]

One of the biggest events held at the pavilion took place in July 1907. Postmaster-General and Minister of Labour, the Honourable Rodolphe Lemieux came to Berlin with his Deputy Minister. These two had just succeeded in framing and getting passed the Lemieux Act, a cornerstone of labour legislation in Canada. The young deputy was Berlin's own William Lyon Mackenzie King. "A large number of citizens, including a galaxy of the fair sex, were awaiting and half an hour was spent in a social manner...and Mr King renewed old acquaintances."[52]

By 1915, the News Record was commenting on the sad state of repair of the pavilion: railings were rotting and footings were weakening. The all-wood structure built on very wet land never had a chance to last decades.[53]

It's World War I in Berlin, Ontario and the pavilion will soon play a prominent role.

*The $8,000 comfort station raised many eyebrows when it opened in 1910. The women's compartment had two rooms: one with toilets and wash-basins; the second, called the rest room, was furnished with settees, easy chairs, rockers and a writing table. Over the years this room was taken out of service. This 1963 photo shows young people in their party best heading for Teen Town, a recreation centre set up in the refurbished rest room.*

## Comfort Station:

The oldest building still standing in Victoria Park opened in June 1910. Two years before, the Telegraph had pointed out that, with no conveniences in the park, visitors had to trek to one of the King Street hotels. On some weekends, the park hosted thousands of excursionists so even with the addition of a few 'earth closets' near Dill Street and at the athletic grounds, the problems remained.

In mid 1909 the Park Board went into action, calling tenders on Charles Knechtel's plans for the site near Schneider Avenue. At a total cost of $8,000 it's not surprising to find the newspapers calling it the finest in Canada. The gray quarry stone, enamelled brick, terrazzo floors and pressed metal ceilings were meant to last. The structure is much the same in 1996 as it was in 1910. Internal fixtures and the lounge area have changed, the original five-cent pay

### Animals at Zoo Ready For Winter

Victoria Park in November is a rather muddy proposition but it is well worth the trip to see the animals of the park Zoo, for this is the time of the year when they are Lat their best. All in their heavy winter fur with that sleek fresh appearance which is lost later in the winter and all out for their last few frolics before retiring for the season, the animals are unusually attractive.

Bruin, whose antics have been watched with great amusement all summer, is now getting ready for his long sleep. The bear house has had a frame building built all about it and the space of about a foot in between filled with leaves. This will make his home quite comfortable and enable him to snore the next few weeks away without being at all disturbed by the wintry weather.

The coons have already gone into seclusion and their pen seems deserted. Curled up in a warm, cosy bed of leaves in a far corner of their house they are already dreaming of the springtime to come.

In the squirrel pen there is great activity. Twenty of them with their big, bushy tails and their heavy coats of winter fur are making merry in the warm sunshine of the afternoons of our late autumn. Four of these squirrels are young ones. Several of the older animals have been killed recently in fights.

The beavers, which during the summer were shy and kept out of sight under the water and, in their underground home, have taken advantage of the fact that they have had few visitors recently and are enjoying themselves in the water and sunning their sleek glossy hides on the bank. The animals are grown to an unusually large size weighing in the neighborhood of 60 to 70 pounds, yet they move through the water with the ease and grace of a small fish. They are becoming quite tame and on sunny days come out in the middle of the afternoon and stay out several hours.

In the deer run and in the bird houses no changes of any kind have taken place but everything is in splendid shape and an excellent opportunity is afforded those who desire to see the animals at their best. The Swans have been taken in off the lake early this season. Last year they were left out and were frozen in a thin surface of ice on the lake and some difficulty was experienced in getting them out safely.

Superintendent Koehler is very fond of the animals and is doing his best to see that they are well cared for during the cold season. When the spring season opens it is thought that steps will be taken to enlarge the Zoo which has become one of the most pleasing features of Berlin's park.

*Berlin Daily Telegraph November 29, 1915*

toilets are gone and the building regulation signs have disappeared:

‘No unusual noises, profane language or disorderly actions.

‘No Smoking. No expectorating upon the walls.

‘No banging on, or climbing over any partitions’[54]

On occasion the Park Board hired help to work part-time, supervising and cleaning the women's section. In 1954, following complaints, the superintendent was told "to engage a janitress on the basis of 3 hours a day, 7 days a week."[55]

As the Park Board and Kitchener Recreation Commission headed towards consolidation in the 1960s, the board offered the old lounge room as a recreation centre. It was outfitted for teens and was known variously as Teen Town or Nirvana. More recently that area has been turned into a Victoria Park museum. That plan isn't new! In September 1920 one Park Board member suggested dismantling the comfort station and turning it over to the Waterloo Historical Society for its artefacts collection. Society president W H Breithaupt's response was lukewarm and nothing further came of the idea.[56]

## Animal Pens:

While the pavilion was rising in the spring of 1902, the area southwest was busy as well. Public donations allowed the Park Board to install a deer run: an area 100 by 200 feet enclosed by an 'invisible' wire fence. The first four inhabitants arrived from Muskoka at a cost of $80 and what an attraction they

*Captured deer came to Victoria Park in 1902 and were kept penned near the present playground site. The original pavilion, left, provides background for this 1911 postcard view.*

Joseph Edward Snyder, grandson of David Schneider, spent much of his boyhood in Victoria Park. He was especially fond of the animals and easily recalls one of the park's earliest employees, Fritz Witte, who died in 1925.

*"I don't think he spoke a word of English. He used to go mumbling away talking to the bears while he was cleaning the cage. If one got in his way he'd shove it with the broom. Those poor bears, living off stale bread."*

*The animals and birds moved to their new enclosure in 1911. A wooden frame building within a wire-fenced area provided them with a comfortable home. A rock-lined pond, hand-mower, Chinese geese and fancy chickens highlight this 1920 photograph by Orpheus Schantz.*

proved to be. Other animal pens were added, housing (then much rarer) squirrels along with porcupines and raccoons. A former Berlin policeman, J Walker, now chief in Sudbury, sent two bear cubs to the park in 1913. A sturdy 12 by 45 by 8 foot cage was built near the comfort station. In 1915 the News Record of April 17 described them as "...lively as crickets, tame and used to surroundings... will come and take things from people's hands."

Several pair of bears lived in Victoria Park over the years but most died after a season or two. One hardy duo got so large and

*Beside the railway tracks where Schneider Creek enters the park an animal and fowl enclosure was built in 1911. A large pond heated in winter allowed a year-round collection of exotic waterfowl to be kept. In this mid 1920s photograph Dorothy Russell captured nine different bird species and an unidentified Park Board employee.*

elderly by 1930 that the board told superintendent Clarence Gress to shoot or sell them. A brief mention of bearskins in the April 30 minutes reveals their fate. That same year a much sturdier bear pen was built along the west shore just upstream from Schneider Island. Here the bears lived for many years until the city's Medical Officer of Health told the Park Board to get rid of them in 1946. Bears made a brief reappearance in the 1950s but beavers were also in this pen for a few years.

Animal and bird donations increased, so the board decided that new quarters were needed. In 1911 a large penned area enclosing a frame structure was built near the stream entrance to Victoria Park. The 'zoo' eventually included eagles, owls, chickens, rabbits, loons, porcupines, deer, peacocks, pheasant, and later, even wolves and foxes.

In winter the heated pond meant the park's clipped swans and wild fowl could stay in the enclosure. Each fall a selection of ducks was fattened on grain and became guests of honour at the annual Park Board duck supper.

As zoos came under increasing scrutiny in the 1970s Kitchener Parks and Recreation, which had replaced the Park Board in 1965, gradually eliminated all its caged animals and tore down the pens.

*In 1968 the maintenance building, kitchen-concession stand and picnic shelter were all in place. Just ending its existence was the busy road which connected Schneider Avenue and Park Street.*

## Roadways:

One of the most common criticisms of Victoria Park is the major road bisecting it. The Courtland-to-Water link began in the earliest years as a park driveway but gradually opened up to automobiles. Theresa and Heins joined only one another, and Park Street ended above the railway tracks. A city plan in the mid 1920s recommended a through road. After several years, and final approval from the Dominion Railway Board, the connections were made and the park was cut in two. Soon it was cut in three. A road from Schneider Avenue swung through the picnic grounds, over the 1921 concrete bridge and was soon hooked up with Park Street. By the 1960s, traffic was so heavy that Schneider Avenue was often fully blocked from Queen Street to the park. The back road was finally closed in June 1968.

Minor roadways once connected the ends of Roland and Schneider (closed in 1955) as well as Water and Richmond, with a branch joining Park Street in front of the Queen Victoria monument (closed in the early 70s).

Park drives have covered the site like a spider-web. Standing at the Courtland entrance, one can still detect a row of trees which lined an early driveway. Another circled the current playground area, west of the pavilion, in the 1930s and '40s. In early photos a majestic drive parallels the row of poplar trees from Heins to Schneider Island.

Traffic experts must hate Victoria Park's lump-like presence on their maps.

*Double entrance pillars at Water Street were installed by Casper Braun in 1908 and look quite new in this overhead postcard view. The park drives were not yet open to through traffic but horse-drawn vehicles and bicycles were popular methods of touring Victoria Park. Seen in the background are Reuben Bowman's 1896 boathouse and William Collard's first ice storage building on David Street.*

Many studies have been done to ease traffic flow. A particularly frightening one in 1964 wanted to extend Park Street straight across the park, over a bridge, and connect it with Schneider Avenue. A 1971 Victoria Park renovation study suggested re-routing all traffic around the park. In 1982, the Region of Waterloo, which by that time managed the Park-Courtland connection, predicted large problems on Joseph, Homewood and West Avenue if the park route was closed.

The subject continues as a topic of heated discussion and <u>will</u> come up again and again in the park's second hundred years.

*West Drive paralleled the lakeshore from the Roos Island bridge to the park limits and was the place to be seen in the family rig. This 1911 postcard view also shows the original pavilion at left.*

West Drive,
Victoria Park

Berlin, Ont., Canada

Lovers Lane in Victoria Park, Berlin, Ont.

*"Would you like to stroll down the lane with me?" was Jack's message to Maud on this 1913 postcard. The Lover's Lane phrase was only a card-maker's whimsy; it occurs nowhere else in Victoria Park literature. Seen from the Courtland entrance some of these trees still outline the old park pathway in 1996. The turned posts at right were installed in 1908. A canvas fence could be strung to separate the athletic grounds from the main park. The Richmond Avenue grandstand is seen at right while the Queen Victoria monument is at left.*

## Bridges:

Victoria Park will soon span the 19th and 21st centuries so a quick study of its bridges is in order: there have been at least ten (five major and five minor).

Schneider Island, now a natural wildlife area, was, until the 1930s, open to park strollers. Two wooden bridges connected it with the shorelines. From the teens until the 1960s another wooden footbridge just west of that island crossed the channel. An open storm sewer ran into the lake from the Michael/Linden Street area before 1913. It drained groundwater from as far as the train station and Margaret Avenue. Where this entered the lake near the present fountain, a rustic bridge carried pedestrians safely across. Another wooden bridge spanned the lake's upper end before 1921 allowing a park drive to cross the creek. As Victoria Park was being constructed in the 1890s, a bridge over the outflow at David Street was also maintained by the Park Board. A temporary bridge appeared in the spring of 1930 as park workers trucked several hundred loads of fill to make Swan Island larger. It's the only time this wildlife sanctuary has been connected to the mainland.

Of the major bridges, the main one to Roos Island has already been discussed. On the opposite side of the island there have been two bridges. In 1902, as the pavilion was beginning to tower over the young park, the need for a bridge to ease access from the island to the pavilion

site was discussed. Seven years later, a railway-style model from the Stratford Bridge Company was installed. A fault soon became apparent. Skaters and boaters complained of its low overhead clearance: many a bump was carried home as a Victoria Park souvenir. In 1928, both ends were raised one foot and the middle was humped by three feet, nine inches. By the 1970s deterioration was so advanced the structure was removed, although the bridge itself did many years work afterwards near Homer Watson Park. Victoria Park visitors and neighbours soon found the dead-end island a nuisance. On June 30, 1988 a graciously curving

*It's probably a Sunday, judging by the clothes John Fuchs, Ronnie Gross and Harold Russell are wearing. The trio poses in 1947 on the fancy wooden footbridge which carried pedestrians across the stream near the concrete road bridge.*

*Until 1913, the Wilmot (Victoria) Street drain brought pollution into Victoria Park's waters. This rustic bridge marked the storm sewer's outlet into the lake. Across the reflective surface the pavilion and maturing trees provide a dramatic vista.*

*Canoeists and skaters shared a common dislike for the original Roland Street bridge – low headroom. When installed in 1909, the 'Railway Bridge' ran level from Roos Island to the south shore. Unwary skaters and boaters had a good chance to smack their heads on the beams. In 1924 Faith White, left, and Dorothy Russell enjoy an outing in Dorothy's own canoe which they had carried from her Schneider Avenue home.*

*Complaints about the low-lying Roland bridge culminated in a 1928 reconstruction: the new-style bridge presented no more head-smacking problems. This 1940 family photo shows Dorothy Russell, son Harold and aunt Sophie Schantz taking a break from their Victoria Park stroll. Notice Dorothy's box camera with which many of the photographs in this book were taken.*

*Dangled delicately from a crane, the new Roland bridge fit its foundations perfectly and soon workers had everything in working order. Patrons of the park were delighted by the new short cut.*

*What a bright sunny afternoon in Victoria Park! Carl Kruse snaps his son Bill standing on the concrete road bridge. The picture taken, the pair undoubtedly headed for the animal pen directly behind Bill. From its erection in 1911 until its removal in the 1970s, the animal and fowl enclosure — the zoo — was one of the park's most popular sites.*

model was installed, built by Kitchener Forging. History records that Alderman Mark Yantzi and longtime park neighbour Dorothy Russell were the first official users.

Upstream, the 1965 fountain bridge, built by Dunker Construction for $4,400 still provides the best vantage point for watching a Victoria Park sunrise. At the western end of the park, a small piece of tarmac is all that remains as a reminder of the roadway and large concrete bridge beside the animal pens. Built in 1921 to carry vehicles from the picnic grounds to the opposite shore, this sturdy bridge doubled in its first few years as a dam for the park's first swimming pool. It did yeomen work until 1968 when the circular route through the rear of Victoria Park was closed. The bridge itself was dismantled in the 1970s.

*One of the most remarkable photographs in the Dorothy Russell collection is this wintertime overview. Taken in 1925 it frames the concrete road bridge, bearpen, Schneider Island and pavilion. Dorothy's husband, Clarke, stood on the disused swimming pool's diving tower to capture the timeless beauty of a Victoria Park winter. The sturdy frame in the foreground was part of the swimming pool dam.*

Pearl McCarley (nee Stahle) feels Victoria Park coursing through her long life. Born in the family home of Joseph Street in 1904, she met her husband Stewart in 1923 on the park bridge. *"The girls were going to have a party and there were no boys...and we came in from Water Street and were crossing the bridge. In the middle...we invited the boys to the party and that's where I met him."*

Stuart "Buck" McCarley later worked in Victoria Park and did double duty as a park policeman.

*"They had a lot of dances at the pavilion. Oscar (Rieck) and him were busy there, oh yeah."*

## Athletic Grounds:

Today, standing at the clock tower and looking across the wide open field to the south, it's hard to imagine a huge enclosed sports stadium with bleachers, grandstand and fences. For those who do remember, it's still possible to hear the ghostly roar of the crowd, the crack of the bat and the cries of the program sellers. Until replaced by Centennial Stadium and Jack Couch Baseball Stadium in the late 1960s, this was the centre of Kitchener's outdoor sports world. Its roots precede Victoria Park by a decade.

*As the 19th century waned, the Toronto Lithographing Company published a series of bird's-eye view maps of Ontario's towns. Berlin's 1893 map provides the best idea of what Lot 17 looked like before Victoria Park was developed. The scale isn't perfect but by extending Courtland and Water into the open fields one has a good idea of the Athletic Club of Berlin's grounds and the original grandstand position. At left, just above the railway bridge over Schneider Creek, is the Atlantic Glue Works buildings and chimney. On Monday, October 2, 1893 a $40,000 blaze levelled the establishment although the chimney stood for another four decades.*

In the 1880s the Berlin Amateur Athletic Association bought five acres of Samuel Schneider's land in the present David-Courtland-Richmond area. They built a wooden grandstand facing north and the grounds hosted baseball, lacrosse, cricket, football (soccer) and tennis. Incurring a large debt in 1893, this group sold out to the new Athletic Club of Berlin headed by David Forsyth, Rev Father Theo Spetz and William Roos. One hundred $50 shares were sold and the money soon made the grounds into what the April 14, 1894 Daily Record called "...undoubtedly the finest in Ontario outside the Rosedale grounds in Toronto." David Forsyth had helped to make Berlin a soccer powerhouse in the 19th century so it is ironic to note that while he headed the Athletic Club, it hosted the area's first contest of the newer rugby football, which eventually supplanted soccer in popularity.

*George "Pop" Philip*

Following its second summer of operation, this group was also losing money. When the newly-formed Park Board expressed interest in buying the facilities there was little objection. The stockholders got their money back and at a cost of $2,500 the Park Board had ready-to-go athletic grounds in use before Victoria Park was even built. Following the 1896 season the board decided to move the grandstand from alongside the newly-excavated lake to the end of Richmond Avenue where it would face east. A conical refreshment stand run by 'Pop' Philip was positioned near the grandstand.

The union of the park and the athletic grounds was the cause of the admission controversy mentioned earlier. Events boiled over in the spring of 1908 during an angry clash between the Park Board and Berlin's iconoclastic mayor, Allen Huber, who claimed the right to control all aspects of the park. Among his edicts was the banning of any admission charges at any time. Quoting the Public Parks Act, the Board soon re-established its rightful authority. A stout canvas fence was erected, stretching from the Courtland entrance to the grandstand near Richmond. When a sporting or musical event was on, the fence was strung from a series of posts and the athletic grounds became isolated from Victoria Park itself.

Many-and-varied activities filled the athletic grounds in the 1896 to 1912 period. Agricultural exhibitions, Dominion Day gatherings, Old Boys' Reunions, carnivals and the July 1912 Cityhood Celebrations were just some of the events Berliners enjoyed at the grandstand. Two specific days give us a good sense of the entertainment.

The Berlin Musical Society band not only played on Roos Island, but put on many concerts in front of the grandstand, using a portable bandstand. A joint Berlin/Waterloo concert on June 30, 1899 featured stirring music and one of the earliest moving picture displays in town. A 'projectoscope' threw a 12 by 13 foot image onto a curtain in front of the grandstand. Still pictures of local dignitaries and movies of horse races and female wrestlers thrilled the crowd. 'Pop' Philip's entertainment didn't stop there: his 'stereoptican' fired a beam of light through a film of water. The insects living in that water were projected in gigantic form onto the curtain. The News Record gushed: "...the public got more for their 10¢ than they ever did before...."

The largest crowd to gather in the athletic grounds was undoubtedly the 12,000 who jammed every corner on September 24, 1908. Prime Minister Sir Wilfrid Laurier, cabinet members and area Liberals basked in the throng's cheers. William Lyon Mackenzie King, candidate in North Waterloo, had recently been a Deputy Minister in Laurier's government, helping to forge some of the world's strongest labour legislation. In his speech, Laurier promised a new cabinet department just for labour and intimated that if Berlin elected its native son, then Mackenzie King would head it. The crowd went wild!

*Mayor Allen Huber of Berlin and the Prime Minister of Canada, Sir Wilfrid Laurier, in their carriage on the way to Victoria Park on September 24, 1908.*

Beginning in 1910 there was much agitation for a modern grandstand and improved facilities. For three years the project was delayed by complex and tiresome meetings, decisions, committees, arguments, decisions, reverses, decisions, legal wrangles and lots of red tape. Tenders for a new grandstand were called, opened, filed, forgotten. Things reached a climax in May 1912. Town Council voted to abolish the Park Board, putting parks operations under its own control. Berlin town clerk A H Millar sought legal advice at Queen's Park and discovered that only an act of the legislature could approve such a step so council withdrew its threat.[57]

Eventually the Park Board did come up with a new-look athletic park: more spacious, more comfortable, more useful. What had been the Bowlby lands, lying along David Street almost as far as Joseph, were incorporated into the new athletic park, making up, in baseball terms, the new right-field area. The grandstand was not replaced: it was instead renovated and moved again. It now faced north from its new position beside David Street. This restructured 1912 athletic park was fully enclosed by a wooden fence and included all the Bowlby land purchase plus some of the old athletic grounds. The remainder of the old athletic grounds was outside the fence and became free-use sports fields. As the automobile became

*Baseball team photos rarely include fans but this early 1920s lineup of the Kitchener Beavers professional club does just that. Everyone, from players to clergy, youngsters to grandparents is wearing a hat and eager for the cry of 'Play Ball.' Holes in the chicken wire meant those seated right behind home plate had to be constantly alert! This is still the original Athletic Club of Berlins' grandstand built in the 1880s. Much refurbished, it had moved twice and now faced north from near David Street.*

more common this field was turned into a parking area during events. Apart from some modifications in 1919 to accommodate a professional baseball team (the Beavers), the athletic park was now in the state in which it would remain until 1952. That year, the oft-repaired, sixty year old, wooden grandstand was finally replaced. A $37,000 debenture issue

*A pair of complementary bird's-eye views of Victoria Park in the late 1890s. From the widow's walk of a Queen Street South home, Albert Snyder captured a crowd attending an event in Victoria Park. His photo tells many stories: the wooden fence along David Street, the Peace Memorial, the grandstand in its Richmond Avenue location, the ticket house at the Courtland entrance and the higher fence surrounding part of the athletic grounds (and advertising the A Weseloh Company). Beyond the Peace Memorial and Kaiser's bust stands the German flagpole, dedicated on August 13, 1897. The earlier Jubilee pole displays the Union Jack near the Courtland Avenue entrance. Otto Kalbfleisch is building his Italianate-style home on the north corner of (the future) Hilda Place and David Street. It is now 79 David Street.*

*In the Denton photo dated 1898 or '99, the photographer has climbed part way up the Jubilee flagpole for one of the most stunning early views of Victoria Park. Pathways and drives wind like a maze over the carefully-landscaped grounds. The Peace Memorial and bandstand are in perfect alignment and Roos Island is centred as if by a draughtsman. Barely visible, where the pathways cross to the right of the Peace Memorial, is the 200 foot deep well providing sulphurous water. Note how all the island elm trees have disappeared after so dominating earlier photos of the park. In the centre background, poking above the trees, is the chimney of the burnt-out Atlantic Glue Works.*

A new concrete grandstand and dressing room facility was constructed in Victoria Park in the spring of 1952. Modern light standards had been installed two years earlier. First and third base bleachers were added over the next few years and the stage was set for this January 1958 aerial view. As a dual baseball-football operation, the athletic park had movable right-field bleachers. Before the winter of '57-'58 set in, the final event was obviously football, attested to by the bleachers located in centre-field. At lower left is the David-Courtland intersection. Note the row of trees which were labelled 'Lover's Lane' earlier. Victoria School at right would lose its tower within a couple of years. Within six years, the Victoria Park athletic park was itself dismantled and removed.

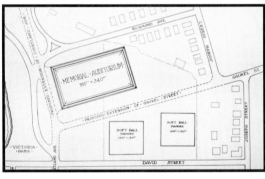

This was one of the 1946 proposals for putting the Memorial Auditorium in Victoria Park. Several variants were suggested until the idea was dropped altogether in favour of the East Avenue location.

When a state-of-the-art lighting system was installed in the athletic park in 1950, the Victoria Park night scene was altered dramatically. A Kitchener-Waterloo Record photographer captured this startling light and shadow effect in 1953 from Roland Street.

For many years Victoria Park's athletic field hosted the annual K-W Labour Day festivities. Tug-of-war battles, athletic prowess demonstrations, music and kids events highlighted the day. Youngsters at this 1963 Labour Day are ready to have their decorated bicycles judged. The baseball press box looms high over the grandstand.

allowed the Park Board to award Dunker Construction the job of building a modern concrete structure and new bleachers.

Concession stands and dressing rooms were built beneath the grandstand while a press box and public address booth soared above it. At long last Kitchener had an ultra-modern sports facility, but it wasn't to last long! Less than fifte

Kitchener schools held many events in Victoria Park. Field days often included non-athletic activities such as this May Day 1938 King Edward School celebration. The May Queen is Nancy Hall, crown bearer is Mary Lou Becker, and the train bearers are Murray Fried and Richard Bader.

*A full house in the athletic park helped celebrate the coronation of King George VI on May 12, 1937. Radio descriptions of the event were relayed to the crowd via the large, mounted speakers. This view from the first-base bleachers along David Street shows the crowd and attending Boy Scouts listening to a speech from a local dignitary.*

years later, demolition crews were stripping the athletic park.

Studies in the 1960s had shown Victoria Park wasn't the best location for a major sports stadium: parking was a problem, equipment costs were rising and Kitchener wanted to consolidate its sports facilities in one large complex. In the run-up to 1967, communities were encouraged to undertake special centennial projects. Kitchener's response was to build Centennial Stadium and Jack Couch Baseball Stadium behind the Memorial Auditorium on East Avenue. Ironically, back in 1946 this same Memorial Auditorium had come close to being placed in Victoria Park's athletic park. Thus, 20 years later, the athletic park made the move to the auditorium!

In its time, the athletic park provided Kitchener with a flexible site for all types of mass meetings. Youngsters poured into the grounds for their annual Field Day. Victory Loan rallies, religious services, Labour Day picnics, civic receptions, union meetings, motion pictures, baton twirling competitions, Fire Department demonstrations, monster bingos, military inspections, professional wrestling – and that's only a preliminary list. In July 1922, Jack Dempsey fought an exhibition match. Generations of Victoria School pupils enjoyed the grounds for their physical education classes; in fact, a special entrance close to Joseph Street was put in just for them. In winter, the Pan Politae Y's Men's Club sold Christmas trees from under the bleachers.

The athletic park portion of Victoria Park is now a memory, a ghost. The large open space is part of the exciting new entranceway from the downtown. With the old City Hall clock tower tolling the hours, with pathways and lights in place, the area that once resounded with the cheers and applause of thousands is a people place again.

*The Peace Memorial, minus its bust, didn't attract a great deal of attention between August 1914 and February 1916. Ernest Denton of the Berlin Portrait Rooms felt there was sufficient interest in the bust-less memorial to offer mounted photos of it for sale in 1915.*

*In addition to rubber-neckers, the pavilion fire on March 24, 1916 attracted at least two photographers. George Lippert of Roland Street and Dorothy Russell of Schneider Avenue each captured the burning building. Four of Lippert's shots are known and five of Russell's survive. In Lippert's scene, Fire Chief Guerin (white coat) climbs the ladder. Stopping on their way to class, schoolboys add interest to Russell's photo of a turret's destruction.*

## "...A SMALL MIRROR: A CLEAR REFLECTION..."

Berlin wasn't the only Canadian community to experience severe racial strife in World War I. But Victoria Park's suffering must be without parallel among the nation's parks. Those problems began even before war was declared.

When the Peace Memorial was unveiled in 1897, women of the German community donated a huge Imperial German flag to the Park Board. During the intervening years it had flown on special occasions from the park's second, or German, flagpole near the Queen's monument. As per British law, it always flew below the Union Jack.[58]

On Sunday, May 27, 1914 vandals tore the flag down and left it lying, mutilated, near the boathouse. The protestors probably didn't realize it had been flying in honour of Empire and Victoria Day.[59]

War between Britain and Germany was declared in early August. Within three weeks the Kaiser's bust had been toppled as detailed earlier. The pedestal of the Peace Memorial remained, bust-less, until

*George Lippert*

Walter Bean was born and grew up in the house still standing at 19 Roland. His earliest Victoria Park memory is of a boot.

*"one morning I woke up, something was wrong... all I could see were firehoses and a fireman's boot. That was the day the Victoria Park first pavilion burnt down."*

A fireman's boot, lost in the rush to get to the fire, and still an indelible memory for the then eight year old boy living beside Victoria Park.

ordered destroyed and cleared in February 1916 following further park trouble.

Waterloo North was committed to raising a battalion of four companies totalling 1,038 men to aid Canada's war effort. The 118th was to have barracks in the Rumpel building at Queen and Courtland. Some of their training would take place beside the athletic park.

Soldiers did more than drill in Victoria Park. The 118th's Bugle Band was given permission by the Park Board in January 1916 to use the shuttered and unheated pavilion for practice sessions. On March 13, 1916 both the Telegraph and Record reported that a detachment was guarding the Queen's monument. Rumours had been making the rounds of an attempt to damage the statue. As the men returned to barracks around midnight a shot rang out, narrowly missing a sentry. The unsuccessful assassin escaped up Benton Street to a waiting fast sleigh.

*Two frames from the May 20, 1916 film by Charlie Roos. 'Pop' Philip's kiosk and the Queen Victoria monument are in the background as men of the 118th go through their paces. Below, dignitaries, including W G Cleghorn (standing in car), hand out gold pieces to the soldiers. Four year old Victoria School overlooks the ceremony while many citizens watch from the athletic park's wooden grandstand and bleachers.*

*Within a month of the fire, Albert Snyder took this photo of the burnt-out pavilion. At right is the kitchen and restaurant area which suffered complete destruction. Much of the undamaged wood was used later in constructing the park residence. Final removal of the foundations took place in July 1918. At left is the old Jubilee flagpole which blew down in November 1914. It had been stored at the pavilion since then but survived the fire.*

On Thursday, March 24 members of the Strome family awoke in their home on Schneider Avenue to notice smoke pouring from the nearby pavilion. Chief Harry Guerin and the Berlin Fire Department received the

Inspector Renbourn of the Ontario Fire Marshal's Office labelled it a case of incendiarism but had no evidence of any particular suspect or motive. He was "...reasonably certain it was not the work of any pro-German... it was the work of someone who had a grudge."[60]

All reminders of the pavilion's existence were quickly removed. Some of the wood, which had originally come from the old exhibition building at Woodside Park, was again recycled in the 1917 superintendent's residence at the end of Richmond Avenue. The pavilion site was completely

*September 11, 1916 was one of Kitchener's most impressive military moments. The Presentation of Colours to the 118th North Waterloo Overseas Battalion took place in Victoria Park. Following consecration services by Rev Capt Andrew, Lieut-Col L W Shannon, O C 1st Military District, unfurled the new colours. The King's colours he presented to Lieutenant E S Hodgins (kneeling, left) and the Regimental colours to Lieutenant G L Ziegler. This postcard view shows Richmond Avenue homes. The earlier scene of the ceremony looks towards David Street, the grandstand and Victoria Public School. In each photograph is seen the cameraman who took the opposite view.*

7:21 alarm and quelled the blaze by 9:00, saving about half the structure. Berlin's two newspapers had quite different angles to the fire.

The News Record mentioned that anonymous letters had threatened damage if specific actions weren't taken by the Park Board. In response to the threats a special constable had been hired but soon released because of the costs. Later writers have stated that those *pro-British* letters demanded the firing of German-speaking park employees, specifically superintendent Barney Koehler. No evidence of these letters or their contents exists in Park Board minutes, archives or other contemporary collections, nor is there any other newspaper reference to them. However, one week later, the Park Board accepted Koehler's resignation, advertised for a replacement, but did in fact keep him on the job for another ten years. The board's action showed there's more than one way to deal with bigotry.

The Daily Telegraph took another tack: it immediately quoted Park Board chairman Daniel Hibner and 118th Commanding Officer W M O Lochead declaring the fire a *pro-German* plot. Their suspicions centred on revenge for the bust-toppling 18 months earlier or anger at the Bugle Band's use of the pavilion.

*The Gaukel Street gasometer looms over this at-ease vignette of the 118th Battalion in Victoria Park on September 11, 1916. Following the Presentation of Colours, soldiers and civilians mingled. The dozen-or-so men in the foreground are members of the 118th's Bugle Band. Their pensive looks underline the fact that the next day they leave for further training at Camp Borden. Alderman W G Cleghorn had led the city name-change proponents in recent months and was close to the 118th's senior officers. He had easy access to military activities to pursue his favorite hobby: photography. As a result his collection is unparalleled in detailing the 118th's existence.*

Perhaps the most memorable day in the 118th's existence was September 11, 1916. The unit was about to leave the city for training at Camp Borden. Following a parade along King and Water, an estimated 15,000 citizens crowded into the park with the battalion. The men were inspected and then the drummers made an altar of their drums. Two veiled flags formed a cross over the altar. Following prayers, they were unveiled and handed over to the colour bearers while the commanding officers made acceptance speeches. The Queen Anne's Chapter of the IODE presented these. The King's was a large Union Jack with the words "118th North Waterloo Overseas Battalion" worked in red and gold. The Regimental's was blue silk with a small Union Jack in one corner and a hand-embroidered maple leaf/beaver/crown design in the centre. The same words were included on this colour.

An impressive March Past thrilled the crowd. The final event was a presentation to each soldier, by the Princess of Wales Chapter of the IODE, of small gift boxes of tobacco, socks and sundries.

This was the last hurrah in Kitchener for the 118th. Some of the men that day had other things on their minds such as desertion. From the letters of Ada Clemens to her cousin Gordon Eby, a 118th officer, "What do you think of your new flags? Will you take those to the firing line when you go? The week after the battalion had left 6 uniforms were found in Victoria Park and I saw about 6 or 8 soldiers coming out of the police station who had overstayed their leave."[62]

The 118th's colours were last seen in public on June 6, 1939. They were flown and lowered at the train station when King George VI made a brief stop. At present the colours are at St Andrew's Presbyterian Church in Kitchener.

Other World War I activities around Victoria Park were less dramatic.

Superintendent Koehler laid out acres of model vegetable gardens near Devon Street in 1917 and 1918. Cabbages, potatoes, onions and such were put in to encourage citizens to participate in the city's 'Home Gardening Project.'

In April 1917 Canada's first Home for Returned Soldiers was established at 113 David Street. Fourteen hundred dollars raised by public subscription bought a two-storey home originally built by A C Quickfall. It was renovated and outfitted to provide a place of rest, rehabilitation and comradeship for men who had returned disabled from overseas duty. 113 David later became a private home again. It was torn down during the mid 1980s rechanneling of the park outlet stream.

cleared by mid 1918 and remained empty until the second pavilion was constructed in 1924.

Spring and summer 1916 saw the 118th in almost daily activity in Victoria Park, much to the delight of neighbourhood youngsters. City Council hired Galt film-maker Charlie Roos to shoot a promotional movie about Berlin, hoping to boost the community's battered national image. On May 20 Roos filmed a parade and drill by the 118th. Also shown was a Victoria Park ceremony in which each Berlin soldier received a $10 gold piece from the city. Alderman W G Cleghorn, substituting for the mayor, was loudly applauded for his stirring address. (Mayor John Hett had been advised by council to stay away because of too much ill-will between himself and the battalion.) Fortunately a copy of this Charlie Roos film still exists: it is the earliest known moving picture of the city to have survived.[61]

1918 would be the war's final year but that wasn't apparent until the fall. In June, the Governor-General, the Duke of Devonshire visited Kitchener. Superintendent Koehler's men constructed a large platform decorated with bunting, allied flags and cedar boughs. Mayor David Gross hosted a huge ceremony in Victoria Park.

In 1918 Canada's Governor-General, the Duke of Devonshire, along with his wife and two daughters, toured the country, boosting the war effort. Mayor David Gross (right) welcomed the vice-regal party to the Twin Cities and led them to Victoria Park. After the speeches and music, and following tradition, his Excellency declared a holiday for all city school children.

Perhaps the final war-related event in the park was the Sunday, August 4, 1918 Remembrance Day ceremony on Roos Island. The IODE and the Great War Veterans Association presented an afternoon of music, speeches and prayers. Reverend Eric Wethey pointed out that the coming world would be much different from what had gone before. Returning soldiers would demand a square deal from those who stayed home.[63]

The war put great strains on the Park Board and especially its superintendent. To reward Barney Koehler for his tribulations he was voted a $50 war bonus in December 1919.

Kitchener was full of ideas for a memorial to the soldiers of World War I. Park Board member A W Feick wanted a tree planted in the park for each fallen soldier. Later there was talk of a monument near the old Peace Memorial site. This would have included the two German field guns given to the city. Yet another idea had a fountain installed with plaques to the dead. None of these proposals was adopted but there *is* a memorial in Victoria Park to some of the men who fell.

On May 6, 1921 principal J F Carmichael and boys from his Victoria School senior class went to Breithaupt Park with superintendent Koehler. Each dug out a sapling, returned to Victoria Park and planted it between Schneider Avenue and the playground. Each tree was dedicated by the student to a special person. Several honoured fallen soldiers: Keith Staebler (grandson of J M) remembered his cousin Eric; Cameron Washburn honoured his brother Robert; Harold Hewitt's tree was dedicated to his brother Albert. Other dedications ranged from school trustee Louis Sattler's recognition of Babe Ruth to Walter Bean's for his late sister Dorothy Belle. Seventy-five years later many of these memorial trees are still growing.[64]

Victoria Park had one further, final, spasm of racial hatred to undergo.

A committee of Kitchener City Council recommended in December 1919 that another vote be undertaken to change the city's name. Hundreds of people, many of them veterans, jammed the chamber, enraged. Aldermen, sensing the mood, voted down the report. Two councillors however, didn't vote: H M Bowman and A L Bitzer. Both were seized by the crowd which tried to make them kiss the flag. Bitzer's attempt wasn't considered good enough. He was frog-marched to Victoria Park for several dunkings in the chilly lake.

The problems that wracked Berlin/Kitchener in the 1914-19 era reflected events elsewhere in Canada. The name-change controversy ensured ours received much more publicity. Likewise the troubles in Victoria Park were just a smaller part of those in the city itself. But a small mirror can capture a clear image: analysis of the Victoria Park problems does give a good reflection of the times.

## "...HE HAS LEFT OUR CITY MORE BEAUTIFUL..."

For less than 12 of its 100 years, Victoria Park was in Barney Koehler's hands. Yet, he left such an impression that in some ways it still is Barney's park.

Bernhard Koehler was born in Nordhausen, Germany in December 1879 to a family with hundreds of years of landscape gardening experience. Learning under the steely eye of his father, Koehler absorbed techniques which came to the fore in Victoria Park.

In 1909 after three years' service in the German navy, Koehler left the old country heading for New York City. A short while later he turned up in Brantford, Ontario, working for the innovative Dominion Canners Limited. But one year later, in 1911, he moved to Berlin and a more appropriate

Joseph Edward Snyder remembers his childhood days spent in Victoria Park during the teens and 1920s. Of Barney Koehler, park superintendent, *"...he didn't like to have anyone mess around with his fish in the park."* This of course, didn't stop Joseph and his pals from setting their lines, baited with rolled-up chunks of bread and trying to catch a carp. *"We would watch for Barney and he'd be coming down the road on the far side of the park... following the roadway around...and we would have to disappear until Barney went past with his little car, then we'd pull in our lines, we might have a fish on it and hightail it down to Albert Street and sell it."*

position as gardener on the A L Breithaupt estate. A small advertisement in the July 4, 1914 Berlin newspapers for a park superintendent caught Koehler's eye. He applied for, and won the job over many others. Work began August 1; war began August 4.

From the beginning there were whispered comments about another German in the park. The supposed anonymous threats to the Park Board during the war have already been mentioned. That story is given some detail in a profile of Koehler appearing in the 1927 book *The Province of Ontario*. The who's-who section is a series of portraits – probably autobiographical - and the Koehler sketch cites these threats.

When the new superintendent took over in 1914, Victoria Park had started to run down. The previous caretaker, Fritz Kruse, had died a year earlier and replacement workers had lost direction. Money was difficult to come by and projects were continually put off.

*Barney Koehler spent most of his waking hours in Victoria Park. At his urging a superintendent's residence and greenhouses were built. Tucked amidst evergreens and magnolias at the bottom of Richmond Avenue, the two-storey stucco building was Koehler's home until his death. From 1926 until 1959, the next superintendent, Clarence Gress lived here with his wife, Annie. They raised two children, Dorothy and Bruce, seen embarking on a park walk in 1937.*

*Two modern greenhouses were built beside the park residence. First Barney Koehler, then Matt Potje, put all their gardening skills (and much of their time) into utilizing every square foot of the greenhouse space. This late 1940s photo shows Matt Potje (left) with superintendent Clarence Gress.*

Koehler brought to his new job a vision of landscapes, terraces, majestic trees and flowering beauty. His monthly, very detailed reports are still inserted in the Park Board minutes books. They show a man with an eye for detail but focused on a larger scheme.

Between 1917 and 1926 Koehler lived in the park residence at the end of Richmond Avenue. From there he kept his hand on the park's development and ran the adjoining greenhouses which provided thousands of flowers each year. Recreation for youngsters caught his attention and Koehler was an early advocate of neighbourhood playgrounds throughout the city. For ten years, he worked without holiday to beautify Victoria Park. Day and night found him tending a garden or pruning a tree. A glowing editorial about Victoria Park's wonders in the Daily Record of June 2, 1923 noted that: "... the natural has not been sacrificed to the artificial... nature does not stand still and one who plans a garden or park must look ahead and visualize the effect. Too much praise cannot be given to Mr Koehler, the genial superintendent (who has) enthusiasm and innate love of beauty, (a) keen sense of artistic values and a deep love of nature."

*Oscar Rieck takes the wheel on a new park truck in this 1920s photograph. His many duties and personality made him one of Victoria Park's most popular employees. Kitchener Parks System is a phrase seldom used and perhaps was only sported by this vehicle.*

In addition to his Victoria Park duties, he and his men trimmed the city's trees, landscaped the collegiate, and developed the hospital grounds. He planned and laid out Kitchener's new Woodland Cemetery.

Tragically, Barney Koehler became an early incumbent at Woodland, aged 47 years. In April 1926 he was driving the park coupe home one evening and failed to see a southbound freight at the corner of Courtland and Stirling. Ten days later he died in hospital.[65]

City Hall was closed for a huge civic funeral. Dozens of tributes were paid and scores of floral wreaths filled the picturesque park residence his widow and two daughters would soon have to vacate. Pallbearers included Park Board members D Alex Bean, A R Kaufman and civic officials. Rev Dr H A Sperling's reading concluded "...he came a stranger to a strange land but he has left our city more beautiful than he found it."[66]

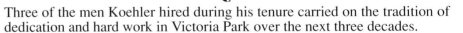

Three of the men Koehler hired during his tenure carried on the tradition of dedication and hard work in Victoria Park over the next three decades.

Clarence Gress began in 1921 as a 26 year old. He brought no formal training in landscaping but learned quickly under Koehler and helped develop techniques for the new tasks park workers were taking on such as ice-grooming and tree-trimming. One year after Koehler's death, Gress became park superintendent, moved into the caretaker's residence and oversaw Victoria Park until 1958. Under Gress the park grew to maturity, major projects came to fruition and a golden age of sorts was reached in the 1950s.

Matt Potje left the horrors of Russian prisoner-of-war camps for the tranquility of Kitchener. He was hired in 1925 to supplement Koehler's own gardening abilities. Over the years, Potje laid out hundreds of imaginative garden designs, not just for parks, but for City Hall, Rockway Gardens and the hospital grounds. Potje's second home was the greenhouse complex which was attached to the park residence. Here, among the humus and potting soils, under the whitewashed glass, he grew and tended the plants which beautified Kitchener throughout the 1920s, '30s, '40s and '50s.

Oscar Rieck began with Koehler in 1917. Or 1921! In an oral history recorded shortly before the 91 year old's November 1994 death, he said spring 1917 was when he began trimming trees for Koehler. Even for those days, 14 seems a bit young. Rieck's obituary starts him in 1921. In either case, he became one of Victoria Park's best known figures. For the park he was a jack-of-all-trades, feeding animals and birds, trimming trees, landscaping, truck-driving and such. Rieck found his real niche after 1939 with the Police Department. Appointed special Victoria Park constable, he patrolled evenings from 7 until 11. At 11 he sounded curfew and everyone left the grounds "...with no nonsense." In winter, the uniformed, beaver-hatted Rieck was on skates keeping order amongst the hundreds enjoying Victoria Park's ice. He admitted it could be rough at times because "...there would be some gangs come down there."[67]

Koehler, Gress, Potje, Rieck. Victoria Park in its third decade was fortunate to have acquired such a dedicated and capable quartet.

# "...RE-STRUCTURING IN THE 20'S..."

As a war-weary Kitchener headed into the 1920s, 25 year old Victoria Park needed revitalizing. Gardens, shrubs and trees were kept well in hand by Barney Koehler and his workers; citizens and visitors flocked to the park in record numbers, yet there were complaints.

There was no pavilion to shelter and feed picnickers and accommodate dancers. As the chorus of criticism grew, the Park Board formed committees, obtained plans, visited other cities' pavilions and called for tenders. Two 1921 ideas promoted a combination pavilion/dancehall/boathouse/bowling alley/refreshment booth structure or a pavilion attached to a 5,000 seat artificial-ice arena beside the athletic park! Finally, in April 1924, Casper Braun's tender was accepted. For $21,600 he promised a completed building by mid-summer. Board chairman Homer Ford turned the sod on April 15 and within four months the official opening celebrated a less dramatic, but more functional pavilion. Architects W H E Schmalz and B A Jones were congratulated on a building in full harmony with its surroundings.

On that August 7th evening, events began with a Roos Island band concert. Around ten o'clock the band and overflow crowd removed to the pavilion. Victoria Park's brand-new lighting system was turned on for the first time that night and the pavilion declared open. The two surviving members of the first Park Board, August Lang and L J Breithaupt were most enthusiastic about Victoria Park's new developments.

The 1924 pavilion was designed with dancing in mind: it was a proven and popular pastime and created revenue. Each year the rights were tendered. Among the people and groups who ran the dances were Fred Mullins and Jack Allen, Carl Halter, the Dominion Rubber Club, H Chace, Wilbur Ott and Carl Gross.

Dancing, however, only filled up a couple of nights each week. What took up the others? Everything from basketball and badminton to bowling and roller-skating; from operas and musicals to square-dancing and talent shows; from archery and soccer-training to card playing and tropical fish shows. The pavilion's basement hummed with the park's workshops where grinders, drills, saws, a forge-and-bellows and hammers repaired and made the tools which kept Victoria Park in shape. Picnickers sheltered in another part of the basement during inclement weather.

The north side of the pavilion originally had a series of French doors opening onto a long balcony with steps leading into the terraced rock garden. As the sweet strains of a dance orchestra drifted over the fragrant flowers, couples could stroll along the pathways and around the lake.

*Homer Ford, chairman of the Park Board, thrust a spade into the Victoria Park turf on April 15, 1924: the new pavilion was underway! Later that spring, Ruth Otterbein of Water Street South took this view of the construction. The west end of the pavilion has changed the most during the intervening 70 years. In 1978, renovations turned it into the main entrance and created a lobby, coat check, and large kitchen.*

*Not as dramatically lovely as its predecessor, the 1924 pavilion was designed to fit the existing landscape. This postcard view (right) by F H Leslie shows how well it complements the grounds. Also from the 1930s, the photo details the north terrace. Wide steps led down from the 6 pairs of French doors. A flowerbed with white flagpole centres the scene while two tennis net posts and some benches show that the lower grounds were well used. The four round brick bays perhaps represent the architects' homage to the original pavilion's design.*

Magic memories of a 1930s dance at the Victoria Park pavilion are easily conjured up.

The most startling transformation in the pavilion's life

took place from December 1941 until late 1945. In aid of the war effort, it was turned over to the Navy League of Canada for the traditional peppercorn rent. Sea Cadets, young men getting their first taste of navy life, trained in a landlocked warship: HMS Warspite. The interior was painted to resemble the quarterdeck of the famous Royal Navy battleship. Various parts of the pavilion represented a wardroom, canteen, mess, library, etc.

Following the war, the Kitchener Recreation Commission began using the basement for offices and the main hall for programs. Several interior renovations have taken place in the intervening years but the exterior retains most of the original look, except for the west end. In 1978 a complete rebuilding of the main entrance and kitchen brought the building up to modern standards. Few nights in the year go by without at least one activity going on in the adaptable pavilion.

With a new pavilion adorning Victoria Park in the late 1920s it became apparent that another of the early park structures would need replacement. Reuben Bowman's 1896 boathouse which sat for 30 years on the David Street shore was rapidly deteriorating. One hundred dollars for 1928 repairs was the final money the Park Board was prepared to spend on it.

Charles Knechtel provided plans and the Park Board opted for a two-storey, double-purpose building near the Queen's monument. About $15,000 was spent and general contractor Steve Becker went to work in April 1929: by late summer the new boathouse was ready. It combined a boat storage-and-rental area, refreshment booth, washrooms and, on the second level, dressing-and-storage rooms for athletic clubs. In winter the boat rental areas were converted into skate changing rooms, strictly divided by sex.

R E Bush had held the Victoria Park boat concession in the old boathouse but passes from the scene as the new one appears. Jess Cole, Art Teevins, Albert Hutchinson, Tommy Gitschner, Kitchener Dairies and others ran the boats and concessions in the 1930 to 1960 period. In more recent times, the canoe and paddleboat rentals, along with a picturesque gondola have been in the hands of Terry Haggith. The boathouse concession, under the name, Jester's Court, is currently operated by Sheila-Marie Biers and George Manolakos.

*Realistically painted to simulate nautical life, the pavilion became HMS Warspite during World War II. At the western end of the dance hall a trompe l'oeil depicted the big ship's massive gun turrets. Around the perimeter of the dance floor a 12 foot high plywood wall portrayed ship convoys, planes, waves, clouds and plumes of smoke. So realistic was the effect that some cadets reportedly became seasick on their first visit to the landlocked training ship! Officers serving the cadets in May 1942 were Sub-Lieut Albert Pearson, bandmaster; Surgeon-Lieut G F Watson; Rev H B Smith, Catholic ship-chaplain; Warrant Instructor William Paris; Sub-Lieut A C Menzies; Commanding Officer Earl Putman; Sub-Lieut Tods Rumpel; Sub-Lieut J R Coghill, paymaster; Rev L A Buckley, Protestant ship-chaplain; Warrant Assistant Instructor Kenneth S Archer. Warspite was dedicated on May 31, 1942 by the Honorable Angus L MacDonald minister of naval services, Department of National Defense.*

The Kitchener Racing Canoe Club had headquarters in the boathouse for about 12 years beginning in 1936. Their evening races and occasional regattas added colour and activity but did cause a problem: music lovers felt their frantic paddling and racing distracted from island band concerts so the club was asked to curtail racing during music hours.

Kitchener's various football teams were using the upstairs dressing-room and shower facilities as early as October 1929. This continued until the K-W Dutchmen left Victoria Park in the mid 1960s.

To provide music for skaters and boaters, a small broadcast booth was set up in the second storey. From speakers mounted on the roof and – after 1953 – on the flagpole/light-standard, the sounds of scratchy 78s wafted across the lake. Bruce Gress, son of superintendent Clarence Gress, spun the discs in the late '40s and '50s. "People always wanted waltzes to skate to," he said, "we never had enough variety because they wore out so quickly." That 1953 flagpole was replaced by a similar one in 1994.

After a 50 year absence, the Kitchener Fire Department returned to battle a Victoria Park blaze. It was February 4, 1967 and the boathouse was on fire! As skaters watched, firefighters beat back stubborn upper-floor flames. Damage was extensive, but springtime renovations brought the boathouse back to life as a

*A classic early 1930s view of the new boathouse seen from the eastern end of Roos Island. Shade trees planted during the Kruse and Koehler years are reaching maturity and park visitors enjoy a sense of the rural in the midst of the city. Fifty years after the postcard view a November 1988 scene reveals the drastic alterations to the original structure and to the city's skyline.*

*Fourteen year old Beverly Winter was walking in Victoria Park around 7 o'clock on February 4, 1967. Passing the washrooms attached to the boathouse she noticed smoke seeping out the window. Quickly alerting concession booth attendant Donna Mucci, the pair's actions prevented any injuries to those in the boathouse. Faulty wiring was the cause of the $17,000 fire. Renovations that spring resulted in a single-storey, more modern-looking structure. While firefighters spent 90 minutes quelling the flames, several hundred skaters continued circling the ice.*

*In the '60s and '70s, high school courses expanded in many directions. Hands-on experience was valued and training in leisure sports led these Grade 12 KWC&VS students to Victoria Park in September 1974. Under teacher Don Panagapka's eye, the essential paddling techniques are mastered before loosing the youthful canoeists on the lake.*

single-storey structure. More extensive modifications in the 1980s revitalized the building: the dock was made accessible to the public, the concession moved to the west end. Soon, even a sit-down restaurant was put in. Further alterations in 1995 brought the somewhat dated washrooms up to standard.

On a cold winter's day of skating, the boathouse with its steaming cups of coffee and hot chocolate continues as a welcome refuge.

## "...WHAT GOOD'S THE WATER..."

After Victoria Park's first winter, 1895-96, when the lake surface was used for horse-racing, skating and cutting ice, the Park Board itself began selling ice blocks from the shore: 10¢ a block, you haul it away. By 1900 an industry had been born. William Collard of Roland Street won a ten year lease at $100 per year. He planned to cut and sell ice either from the shore or from a large ice storage shed he proposed erecting on David Street (where 101 David is now located).

From 1900 to 1905 Collard cut and sold thousands of tons of Victoria Park ice while always having to contend with those who favoured skating over cutting. An uneasy truce settled over the ice each winter: luckily no one ever drowned. Walter Bean, whose father D Alex Bean operated the Berlin Daily Telegraph, still tells a story of the days when his father walked across the ice to his downtown office. Returning after dark one night, he forgot where the ice-cutters had been working and plunged into seven frigid feet of water. Luckily he managed to climb out and rush to his home at 19 Roland.[68]

To get large ice chunks from the lake to his storage shed, Collard built a tower-and-slide contraption beside the boathouse. In 1904 the resulting blockage of David Street was the subject of a lawsuit by a neighbour, Jacob Shoemaker. By 1905, Collard tired of the business and sold the remainder of his lease to A C Quickfall.

Quickfall was a versatile entrepreneur: contractor, teamster, carpenter, brick-maker, but he was best-known as the Victoria Ice man.

Quickfall cut ice for the next two decades, often having to contend with tricks of weather such as a freak 1918 winter rainstorm which wrecked the ice yield. Tricks of another kind killed his ice business in the 1912-15 period. Pollution of the most disgusting kind crept into Victoria Park lake via the old open storm sewer running down from the Victoria Street North area. Effluent also flowed in from upstream Schneider Creek businesses such as butchers, glue-makers, and the Hydro-Electric plant on Factory Road (West Avenue).

*William Collard of Roland Street was Victoria Park's first ice harvester. He built this ice storage building where 101 David now stands and his delivery wagons purveyed ice blocks in the summer. The first storage house was enlarged before being replaced by A C Quickfall's larger building in 1913.*

*The only known photograph of ice-cutting in Victoria Park. It's around 1905 and Collard's enlarged ice house is at left with the original park boathouse at right. The lake's floodgate can be seen but its form is lost in that of the tower-and-slide ice conveyance.*

Ice-cutting ended in Victoria Park with A C Quickfall's death in 1927. By this time the Park Board had become fully committed to skating and hockey on the entire ice surface. Techniques for clearing, scraping and flooding had been developed and the surface soon became renowned for its size and smoothness.[70]

❧

When summer's hot, the water's cool. That inescapable fact meant that Schneider Creek and Victoria Park attracted swimmers from its earliest days. The Schneider family record contains many recollections of 'old swimmin' holes' at several locations on the creek. The Schneider sawmill pond, located in the present picnic ground area, was fondly remembered by many old-timers when Joseph M Snyder was collecting

*Albert Charles Quickfall was one of Berlin's busiest businessmen. In 1913, when this family portrait was taken, the new house at 101 David Street had just been completed and the newest child, Eileen, was one year old. Clark, Edith (nee Shoemaker), Eileen, Evelyn, Pearl and A C Quickfall made up one of the many successful families who chose to live on the borders of Victoria Park.*

Each year water samples were sent to the Provincial Health Officer in Toronto. Often these proved the lake water was too vile to use, even for cooling-ice. Arguments went back and forth but when the PHO spoke there was no choice. Quickfall would lose the ice and the Park Board would lose its revenue from Quickfall.

In 1913, despite the setbacks, Quickfall tore down the old Collard storage shed and built another, larger one behind it, halfway between David and Queen Streets. Then he built the stately home at 101 David designed by his wife Edith. For many years after the family sold 101, it was still known as the Quickfall house.[69]

Eileen Dahms, daughter of A C and Edith Quickfall, grew up in 101 David Street. Her childhood memories of the 1920s are mixed.

*"I had the delightful task of answering the telephone, taking orders. I hated it, my summer holidays sitting beside the telephone taking ice orders. They had these flat-bottomed, horse-drawn drays and huge ice tongs that they would take the pieces of ice off and deliver them."*

There was one modern appliance missing from the Quickfall home:

*",,,we didn't even have a refrigerator at our house, we had a wooden box in the basement. That's where our piece of ice was and where mother kept the food."*

*Winter Carnivals attracted thousands to Victoria Park in the 1920s. All eyes are on this couple's showmanship at the 1925 edition and among the crowd was Dorothy Russell who took this view towards the downtown area. Once the lake had frozen a tall wooden pole was inserted through a hole and frozen in place. From it, lights and pennants were strung from guy wires.*

information in the 1920s.[71]

There was no plan for any kind of swimming hole or pool when Victoria Park was on the drawing board in the 1890s. At a 1901 Park Board meeting it was suggested a bathhouse be built along the lakeshore but nothing came of that.

Enter Dr J E Hett. One of Berlin's most interesting characters, Hett held many civic posts including mayor. His first pool plan came in 1908-10. The Park Board would buy an acre of land between the two sets of railroad tracks above the park, dam the creek and create a pool. Nothing resulted.

In 1915, John Hett is mayor. As such he sits on the Park Board and during the April 20 meeting unveils his latest plan. At the eastern end of Roos Island, near the cannon, a portion of the lake 100 by 50 feet would be cut off with a concrete or wood foundation in the water. A canvas fence would be strung along this foundation for privacy and a dressing room built on the island. At the very next meeting, board members rejected this plan, opting for more study at the park's upper end.

The Daily Telegraph, whose editor D Alex Bean of Roland Street would have looked at this monstrosity from his front porch, declared " Victoria Park becomes stagnant in the summer. (It)would marr the beauty of Berlin's finest park (if this) abortion of a public building (went up)."[72]

*Dr J E Hett*

The area between Theresa Street and Schneider Island was proposed in 1918 as a good location for a large concrete swimming tank. Underground springs could provide sufficient water; however the $17,000 cost was prohibitive.

Plans finally came to fruition in 1921. A new

concrete bridge was constructed over the stream at the upper end of the park and a floodgate was built into it. A swimming hole was dug out, lined with wood and then gravelled – Victoria Park had its first, indeed the city's first, public swimming pool. Not surprisingly, pollution and health hazards forced it to be closed within three years.

A Kitchener Swimming Pool Committee was formed in the late 1920s and several sites came under scrutiny. Surveys

*Following World War II, winter carnivals again found an audience. Future mayor Sid McLennan took this January 1948 snapshot of youngsters in the costume skating contest.*

*Over the decades several attempts have been made to separate hockey players from skaters. This well laid out rink in the north channel kept the puck out of the general skating area. On fine winter days in 1951 this rink might hold teams of up to 40 players each.*

*D Alex Bean*

were made, stakes driven in and excavation was just days away. The new Municipal Swimming Pool would be in Victoria Park adjacent to the pavilion and comfort station. Neighbours were incensed, petitions raised, delegations formed, lawyers retained. Still, the plan almost went through, and would have without the largesse of Park Board member A R Kaufman. At the last moment, the pool site was switched to its present Woodside Park setting. Kaufman donated substantial money to grade the land and make it suitable for the large pool and companion buildings.[73]

*How many times over the years has a tractor pulling a scraper-ful of snow plunged into the frigid waters? Luckily, ice is weakest at the shore! There's no rush to get to school on January 9, 1953 for these youngsters as they gather to watch superintendent Clarence Gress (left, fur hat) direct rescue operations. In the background are three Roland Street homes which at one time belonged to Park Board members: at left D Alex Bean's, then Karl Mueller's two-and-a-half storey, 1897 residence and the white-verandahed house of George Lippert. On the other side of Lippert's is the turn-of-the-century home of lake-excavation-foreman and, later, ice harvester, William Collard. The scraper seen here in the water was developed in the Kitchener park organization to meet Victoria Park's special needs. Long time Park Board employee Ken Shiry drives the 30s vintage tractor with a scaper across the park's ice surface. This January 4, 1965 Record photo also gives a good view of the athletic park.*

Best Wishes from Berlin

Victoria Park Berlin, Ont.

for Victoria Park Berlin, Ont

Front Elevation

C. Knechtel. Arch. Berlin

*The earliest colour views of Victoria Park come from the Golden Age of postcards, roughly 1900 to 1930. These were artificially tinted in the publishing process but do give us an added dimension of enjoyment. Two of A S Green's views from the park's opening week were still being used to make postcard scenes two decades after the event. Architect Charles Knechtel showed the Berlin Park Board this watercolour sketch on September 13, 1901. It won the board's approval and Knechtel was awarded the contract to design the park's first pavilion. Since then, this watercolour had been hanging in a Courtland Avenue West home until discovered in July 1996 by Mrs Patricia (Knechtel) Perrett, the architect's granddaughter. She was presented with it by Mrs Emilie Scholtz who had purchased the home from the Knechtel estate decades earlier.*

Victoria Park, Berlin, Ont.

*For the 1912 celebration marking Berlin's cityhood, car and motorcycle owners were invited to a rally in Victoria Park. From the top of the pavilion, this is the scene looking towards Park Street. At Barney Koehler's suggestion, a caretaker's residence was built inside the park at the end of Richmond Avenue. Much of the wood used in its construction in 1917 came from the undamaged portion of the burnt-out pavilion. A 1951 view taken of skaters by Albert Fuller triggers golden memories for many who remember mid century in Victoria Park. Ellroy Lippert served on the Park Board and was park administrator in the 1950s and '60s. An avid photographer, he caught this stunning scene in 1955 following a severe sleet storm.*

Winter carnivals under several names have been a Victoria Park tradition since the early 1920s. Snow sculpturing knows no age barrier and kids such as Adrian Haldenby have as much fun as experienced artists.

A little touch of Venice was introduced to Victoria Park in 1991. Terry Haggith imported an authentic Italian gondola and has raised more than a few eyebrows. Among his first guests were Kitchener's longtime mayor, Dom Cardillo, and aldermen Mike Wagner and Carl Zehr.

Hot air ballooning has really caught on in the 1990s and the old athletic park area makes an ideal launching field. The colourful balloons catch everyone's attention as they lift off gracefully then soar out of sight, usually in a southeasterly direction.

The biggest annual attraction in Victoria Park is the Multicultural Festival held each Canada Day weekend. Food vendors set up dozens of tents and the visitor can sample a United Nations of the palate. On Roos Island displays of crafts and products bring the world to Victoria Park. Entertainment from Africa, the Caribbean, Europe, Asia and the Americas drive pounding rhythms throughout the park. Tens of thousands of people jam Sam Schneider's old farmland for one of the city's premiere events.

*November 1995 saw Victoria Park burst into colour! Some 35,000 light bulbs sprinkled Christmas cheer throughout trees and structures. Each evening hundreds of people strolled the park marvelling at the ever-changing scene. Fourteen service clubs joined forces to get the lighting project off the ground and the result exceeded everyone's hopes. An unexpected side effect was the drastic slowdown in traffic as drivers took in the colours and vistas.*

*Take an early morning sun, a steel-blue sky, a few Victoria Park trees, let them play together, then press the camera button. This 1991 scene is gone forever. The willow, one of the park's largest trees, was removed after crashing to the water in the autumn of 1995.*

*From Roland Street, across the shore and lake, onto Roos Island — the eye takes in a riot of colour and flora. Compare the 1996 scenery with A S Green's view of the island taken from the bridge a century before.*

IV

But a pool did come to Victoria Park. In 1952, the Kitchener Young Men's Club helped fund the wading pool built near the pavilion. Arguably the park's most popular attraction with the under-eights, it has served well for 45 years.

Unofficially, Victoria Park lake has been a pool for generations of youngsters. In hot summer months as far back as 1909 complaints were made about boys (and men) bathing in the lake. Police were often called to put a stop to the practice. In 1921 shortly after the concrete bridge pool opened, Kitchener was hit by one of its hottest spells of all time. The new pool was jammed. Hundreds more took to the lake itself. While Mayor Charles Greb hinted his approval, Park Board chairman Homer Ford absolutely forbade it. The police were caught in the middle. Tempers flared, but as nature tempered, the lake again became the preserve of ducks and swans.[74]

Even in recent years, it isn't too unusual to spot a youngster or two beating the heat in the tepid waters, this often happening in the midnight hours.

*Before the second summer of swimming began the Park Board had moved a tin shed (previously used by skaters) beside the pool so swimmers could change with decency. In the first summer boys had changed where they might while girls were provided with a tent! In this 1923 photograph many youngsters sit on the dam and bridge between their dips in the pool. A wooden deck has been constructed between the change-house and the pool.*

*Opened in 1921 the Victoria Park swimming pool was a popular spot from the very beginning. At left is the animal enclosure. The concrete road bridge with pool dam is in the centre. The lack of a change-house dates this postcard view to that first summer.*

*July 1, 1963 was a bright sunny day and the Victoria Park wading pool had its full share of young celebrants. How the pavilion landscaping has changed since the 1930s! The flagpole is gone, a rock garden has been installed and shrubs nearly obscure the building's western end.*

*Before World War I the local band was called the Band of the 29th Regiment. All members were civilian volunteer musicians but were given uniforms and had to attend camp once a year and participate in other military events in town. At the turn-of-the-century regular band concerts were given at the downtown bandstand near Market Square, on Roos Island's picturesque bandstand and from a portable bandstand in the athletic park. That's where this photo was taken around 1910. The chimney of the Gaukel Street coal-gas plant gives the site away. An ice cream vendor's umbrella at left promises pleasure to both young and old. When World War I broke out, the 29th became the 108th and the musicians accompanied the locally-raised 118th North Waterloo Battalion throughout 1915-16.*

Doris Huber's early remembrances of Victoria Park in the 1920s and '30s centre on music. She and her parents went to the park most Sundays to sit *"...not on the island where the bandstand was, but facing it on the mainland...lots of mosquitos. Later I went with friends and walked in a circle around the mainland, we'd venture onto the island to see what friends we could pick up."* She and her sister, Norma, remember winters being longer and colder and *"..we skated right around the island."* Norma's fondest memory is of the hot stove glowing in the skate-changing rooms at the boathouse and *"...the counter where you could buy, mostly candy, chocolate bars."*

# "...HARMONY AND NATURE..."

There's music in the park! Concert marches, swirling pipes, grand opera, gospel sing-alongs, traditional jazz, rock, country, torchlight tattoos – the list of musical styles and performances held in Victoria Park over 100 years would satisfy the taste of any music lover.

Whether on the Roos Island bandstand, in front of the athletic grounds grandstand, in the pavilion or on a portable stage in some shady corner, music and Victoria Park were made for each other.

No group has played in Victoria Park as often as the Berlin/Kitchener Musical Society band. It could be called the park's own and that's doubly true now with the band headquartered in the pavilion.

The Berlin Musical Society established itself in 1876 with musicians from several smaller Berlin groups. Entering competitions throughout Ontario, it made a habit of first-place finishes. By 1879, the Musical Society band had become the Band of the 29th Infantry Regiment, the local militia unit. During World War I the regimental number was changed to the 108th. In the 1920s the band proudly accepted the name Band of the Scots Fusiliers. Military designations were dropped in 1947 and the band was simply called the Kitchener Musical Society band. Under its varied names, this band has ushered in almost every important event in Victoria Park.[75]

Opening Day: August 27, 1896! The Band of the 29th Regiment was there. Even before that official opening the Roos Island bandstand was inaugurated on August 13 with a concert of marches, overtures and waltzes under bandmaster William Forder.

Queen Victoria's Diamond Jubilee was celebrated June 22, 1897 around the world wherever the Union Jack flew. Here in Berlin the 29th led a parade of schoolchildren into the park to dedicate the Jubilee flagpole erected near the Courtland Avenue entrance.

The unveiling of the Peace Memorial on August 13, 1897 attracted dozens of singing societies and bands from across Ontario, but leading the way up to the Kaiser's bust was the 29th. Five years later, almost to the day, August 15, 1902, Noah Zeller was at the podium as the band played a lively selection from the floor of the just-opened pavilion. A month later the 29th was in top form as 3,000 labour delegates came to the park to support striking workers of the H Krug Furniture Co.

Civic, Dominion, Labour, Empire: whatever the holiday was called, Berlin's band was sure to be on the scene in Victoria Park.

J H Stockton took over the baton from Noah Zeller in 1913 and saw the band through the turbulent World War I years. In 1918 a young man already well-known in Kitchener musical circles began playing a prominent role.

George H Ziegler, born in 1889, came from a multi-talented musical

*Public donations raised several hundred dollars in July 1896 to erect a decorative bandstand on Roos Island. The first concert took place on August 13 with the Band of the 29th Regiment doing honours. In its first incarnation the bandstand's steps led east or west and this photo from the first decade of the park shows a group of ladies having a chat.*

Sometimes crowds were so large the island bridge had to be closed. There was danger of collapse if too many stood on it enjoying the music.

There must have been many magical moments during the afternoon of September 15, 1903. The 29th, again under Zeller, welcomed the Band of the Coldstream Guards of London, England, to Berlin. The 29th serenaded the visitors in front of the Walper Hotel, then accompanied the legendary band to Victoria Park where 2,000 people witnessed a stirring display of precision music. A tidy profit swelled the Berlin Musical Society's treasury.

The 29th helped the IODE raise money for the statue of Queen Victoria in 1907-08. It was only fitting that in May 1911 when the drapery fell away revealing the bronze figure, the 29th should be playing the National Anthem.

The public just couldn't get enough music in the park. Weekly events weren't sufficient; soon both Thursday evenings and Sunday afternoons became standard concert times.

*Following years of complaints of bad acoustics and too small a floor space, the bandstand was given a facelift. The steps on either side were removed and a single set now faced the bridge. An apron extended beyond the original dimensions allowing all band members to be seated. Electric lights were installed and later, a PA system was added with speakers in the gables. The 108th Regiment band opened the new-style bandstand on July 19, 1917. This sylvan scene photo was taken nearly thirty years later, in May 1946, when once again criticism was aimed at the inadequate structure.*

*The 1985 replication of the original structure was designed to serve as more than a bandstand. Its four sets of steps and lower profile are the major differences from the 1896 model. Winter, fall, spring and summer it attracts visitors.*

*World War II put a hold on most Victoria Park capital improvements but agitation for a new bandstand began early in 1946. By spring 1950 a $3,500, 34 foot square structure was ready on Roos Island. Every Thursday evening and Sunday afternoon throughout the 1950s and '60s George Ziegler led the band at its new Victoria Park home. Drummers Jim Fulton and Doug Frey stand at left while trombonist Don Jukes can be identified at the right. Judging by the newness of the bandstand this is probably the summer of 1950.*

family. His famous Conservatory of Music had been established in 1913 and his students began leaving their marks on Canadian music. In 1925, when Stockton retired, Ziegler began a 42 year stretch as conductor of the Kitchener Musical Society band. By any yardstick, his legacy of music is unequalled in this city. The best way to gauge his achievements is with Sybil Crawford's life of Ziegler in the 1988 Waterloo Historical Society Annual Volume.

In addition to the regimental bands, Ziegler fronted several other organizations. All played in Victoria Park. His various Boys' Bands of the pre-Second World War era are still remembered by those who saw them win many awards, most notably at the annual CNE competitions. Even more famous was the Kitchener Ladies' Band of the late 1920s. Numbering at times over 90 members, many of them graduates from Ziegler's

Conservatory of Music, the ladies spread Kitchener's name across the continent.

Kitchener's only outdoors Grand Opera was July 28 and 29, 1938 in the Victoria Park athletic park. Ziegler helped train local participants for I Pagliacci and Cavelleria Rusticana. Thousands enjoyed the touch of Old World culture amidst a baseball field atmosphere.

George Ziegler retired from the Kitchener Musical Society podium in 1967 and died in 1981. The 'home band' has had several conductors since including Arthur Freund, Ray Sweezey, Ben Scott, David Howell, and the present bandmaster Paul Schalm, whose Monday night rehearsals in the pavilion keep the band in top form. Concert appearances by the all-volunteer band are not as frequent in Victoria Park as during earlier decades, but when scheduled, always attract a faithful and welcoming crowd.

In the Roaring Twenties, nothing roared as loud, musically, as the tattoos and carnivals put on in the athletic park by the Kitchener Musical Society. Five or six thousand people would jam the bleachers for music, fireworks, parades, tableaux vivants, vaudeville acts and speeches.

When the large, square bandstand on Roos Island was torn down in 1985 and replaced with a smaller replica of the 1896 original, the role of music changed also. A much more intimate setting was possible, so smaller groups began booking the site. A five-piece Dixieland combo, a pair of Peruvian wind-pipe artists, a chamber group, or a lone singer with acoustic guitar could bring musical magic to a park audience. The annual

*Among the most popular bands in the province during the late 1920s was George Ziegler's Kitchener Ladies' Band. Their appearances in Victoria Park always drew enthusiastic crowds. At this SRO gathering on September 18, 1927 a concert highlight was the vibraphone duet featuring Elizabeth Ziegler and Catherine Holly.*

*Close up, on stage! It's 1952 on the Victoria Park bandstand and George Ziegler conducts the Kitchener Musical Society band for the 27th consecutive year. Joining Ziegler in this photo are Wilmer Strome playing clarinet in the foreground. He spent 66 years in the band. The trombone soloist is Don Jukes; at Jukes' elbow is Harvey Gleiser; in the front row of trumpet players are Ron Frey and Ed Bihun; the second row has an unidentified player at the left, then Jack Ricket, Mike Wagner and Alf Tilby; trombonist John Smith is seated in the back row. At the time of writing, Smith has served 57 years and is still going strong. Tilby was a 56 year veteran when he retired. Gleiser's career continues in the Wellington Winds. The love of music has run long and deep among members of the Kitchener Musical Society, Victoria Park's "own band."*

*Concert band enthusiasts weren't the only ones enjoying music from the Roos Island bandstand. Rock 'n' roll bursts on the scene in the 1950s and '60s. By the '70s all-day rock concerts were attracting thousands of (predominately, but not exclusively) young people to the island. The Record's headline on July 10, 1973 read 'Rock echoes at staid old park' The day before, a Musicanada festival featured such groups as Amish, Whitehorse, Poverty Train and performers such as John Constant and Jonathan Kramer.*

Multicultural Festival imports world music each Canada Day weekend. Of course there's electricity available and that means amplifiers. Day-long festivals featuring several rock groups or blues artists have become popular and Roos Island is the perfect place to escape the city in a blast of musical wattage.

Whether it's a full-size concert band sending toe-tapping marches across the lake, a reggae band pulsating the air with rhythm, or a lone cardinal welcoming the early morning sun, there's always music to be heard in Victoria Park.

❧

Victoria Park has long been a haven for both the true nature lover and the citizen who just wants to escape urban life for a few precious moments. Today mature shade trees outline and border the lake, while century-old

*On the picnic shore, two young ladies in August 1945 wade in the water to feed the ducks and swans. The same scene could be shot today except dozens of gulls would be hovering, waiting for the bread crusts.*

*Fifty years old when Bert Williams took this artistic view in 1945, these Norway Spruce are celebrating their centennial along with Victoria Park in 1996. In the background are the comfort station and the pavilion. The ploughed drive leads into the park workshops in the basement of the pavilion.*

pines create a special atmosphere around the pavilion. Generations of youngsters have climbed the willows and swung, Tarzan-like, over the water. Impressive elms once dotted the park but they were decimated in the 1960s by Dutch Elm disease. Some stately vase-shaped elms are seen in very early photos of Roos Island. They died within a couple of years from too much moisture as the park's water-table rose. There have been continuous tree plantings from the very beginning. A line of 50 fast-growing poplars, planted in 1900, is visible in many Victoria Park photos right into the 1930s. These marked the park's original northwestern boundary, the line of Samuel Schneider's Lot 17 continuing from Frank's Lane. In October 1911 over 200 maple , butternut, elm and walnut saplings were planted by park staff.

In 1949 the Kitchener Daily Record interviewed local naturalist Frank Schantz who identified 55 varieties of trees and shrubs within the park. Today, 1996, Parks and Recreation horticulture supervisor Ted Potworka counts 142 varieties, including such rarities as tulip trees, yellowwood and eastern red bud.[76]

Apart from adding beauty in summer and fall, the park's tree collection has provided incalculable numbers of school children with a wide variety of leaves and nuts for nature projects.

*Nothing symbolizes Victoria Park as much as the swan. The Royal Mute swan has graced the lake from the earliest days. Some years the cob and pen successfully raise cygnets, patrolling the lake with increased vigilance. Their young grow almost visibly from fluffy fist-sized hatchlings to full-sized, though ungainly, year-olds. A 1987 storm has raised water levels drastically but the spray fountain still gushes.*

*The Great Blue heron has increased in numbers and visibility over the past decade and Victoria Park has attracted its share. Up to four of the voracious fish-catchers can be seen in various corners of the park. These urbanized heron have cast off their wilder relative's shyness and will even allow canoeists to pass within a few meters. A favorite fishing ground is the shallow waters around Swan Island where Paul Widmeyer captured this profile in 1989.*

Birds enrich Victoria Park and have done so since 1895. Even in the park's planning stages, they were a consideration. One island was set aside strictly for nature while Schneider Island became a second sanctuary around 1930. Generations of ducks, geese and swans have nested and hatched their young on these two islands. On September 13, 1895, during William B Hewitt's celebration picnic, everyone cheered the fly-by of a single wild duck. Today, its mallard cousins live year-round in Victoria Park, providing delightful entertainment as they scramble for food scraps or huddle together in winter's shrinking black water gaps. Canada geese have been enjoyable on-and-off park residents. Any who wish to stay and raise a family do so at the whim of the current male swan, the cob. In spring and fall, the lake is a handy migratory stop-off for geese and several varieties of ducks.

The swan is emblematic of Victoria Park: George Ricker's 1894 verbal report mentioned the swans; an island was named after them; and by 1903 the park had both white and black species. Various cities, firms and individuals sold swans to the Park Board but in 1925 the first official Royal Mute was shipped from England.

While providing a handsome and educational asset to the park, the cobs

*One real fishing rod, a pool of murky water, the eternal fisherman's optimism: that's all it took on August 31, 1956 to attract ten boys to the concrete bridge in Victoria Park. Note the deterioration in the structure caused by an ever-increasing traffic load. Within 13 years the bridge would be closed. Compare the lights used in 1956 with those in the 1949 photo.*

and pens have sometimes become too aggressive. They've actually chased people who approach the cygnets too closely. In return some people have struck back, wounding or killing a swan. As non-indigenous birds, Victoria Park's swans, like all mutes in North America, must be clipped when young so they cannot escape into the wild. A small wing bone is pinioned by a veterinarian when the cygnet is days old. During winter, the park's swans are captured and sent to a sheltered pen where open water and food are provided. Any year-old cygnets are usually traded or sold to other park systems or wildlife centres. Even direct offspring are treated as enemies by the adult pair when a new mating season arrives.

Because of the park's semi-natural areas and the adjacent, seldom-cleared railway lands, many other forms of wildlife (some welcome, some not) have found their way to Victoria Park. Muskrats proved an early pest, burrowing into the embankments around the lake, causing several collapses. Joseph Kesselring was hired by the Park Board in November

*From front to back, George Rieck, Robert Rieck, Harold Urich and Jim Rieck wait for the big one to bite. In this mid 30s photo taken along the Roland shore the white-columned pergola can be seen in the background. The Rieck boys were sons of park policeman Oscar Rieck. Their disregard of Victoria Park's "No Fishing" rule brought them a severe scolding from dad that evening.*

Lucile Schenk met her future husband, Wally Rieck, when both worked part-time in Victoria Park. Lucile's uncle, Walter Mussleman, ran the concession stand at the bridge in the late 1930s and she earned 15¢ an hour working for him. Wally helped rent the canoes at the nearby boathouse. Lucile's parents had a grocery store at the corner of Benton and Courtland. On Thursday evenings, band concert time, her dad *"...even kept the store open a little later...to do a little extra business with people walking past the store down to the park for the concerts."* In the photograph of the Rieck boys fishing in Victoria Park, Wally isn't in the scene because *"...he was downtown buying more fishhooks."* Lucile recalls Wally's story of all the boys being *"...made to go to superintendent Gress and apologize."*

1899 to cull the muskrat and mink populations. Descendants of those muskrats are still active participants in Victoria Park's wildlife parade. Field mice, rabbits, raccoons, chipmunks, skunks, turtles, garter snakes and several types of squirrels are other fairly common park visitors especially noticeable around dawn and dusk.

Apart from many common bird species, a keen observer might sight owls, hawks and kingfishers. Two members of the heron family, the Great Blue and the Black-Crowned Night, have become regular inhabitants over the past decade. To the chagrin of many, gulls have congregated in massive numbers since about 1970. In 1994, while watching the gulls' antics, Dorothy Russell recalled going to the park around 1912 and staring, amazed, as flock upon flock of migrating warblers visited Victoria Park.

Where there's water (no matter the quality) there are fish and Victoria Park lake is no exception. Carp, suckers, shiners and other coarse fish somehow survive predators and annual drainings to tempt young anglers each summer.

Victoria Park plays a role, unintended and unrecognized, in helping city youngsters come to grips with nature's way. From the often-cruel mating rituals of mallards to day-old fluffy ducklings; from collecting acorns and leaves for school to watching a heron nab a struggling fish; from the ballet-like displays of mute swans to the gulls' feeding frenzies, young people can learn a lot about nature from the wildlife of Victoria Park.

## "...DON'T BLAME THE PARK..."

The roots of vandalism and crime in Victoria Park reach back to the earliest days. A catalogue of mischief in the park could span the century.

*"Refreshment Booth Broken Into," "Nails Sprinkled on Bike Track," "Man Hugs Women Strangers," "Bicycle Stolen," "Youngsters Yell Profanities."*

Sound like headlines from today's Record? Each incident, and many more, happened before the park turned five years old![77]

Such problems are not unique to Victoria Park, to Kitchener or to Canada. The essential features of a Romantic Landscape park create conditions which can nurture criminal activity: dark corners, bushy gardens, many hiding spots and escape routes, and, at times, few people around to spot trouble.

Animals and birds have borne a considerable amount of suffering: stones thrown at ducks, swans maimed with oars, slingshots fired at caged squirrels and black bears poisoned.

Gardens and trees attracted thieves and vandals: 50 Lady Washburn geraniums stolen in June 1917, birch trees stripped of their bark in August 1911, and young pines cut off near the ground, always during December.

The litany of damage could go on and on. Apart from the Kaiser-toppling and pavilion-burning, serious criminal activity had been rare. But in the 1980s a series of attacks, and two murders, made Victoria Park synonymous with danger in some people's minds. Homosexual activity in the comfort station and in the woods beyond the park's boundary became a cause célèbre when events exploded into newspaper headlines.[78]

That mid 1980s period, as horrible as it was, did have a silver lining. About that time, area residents began taking a more active interest in 'their' park. Their increased presence in the daily life of Victoria Park with more events, more strolling, more patrolling and more vigilant eyes helped 'Take Back the Park.' This, combined with upgraded efforts by Waterloo Regional Police and Kitchener Parks and Recreation, started making the park less interesting to the criminal and vandal.

Bad things do still happen: they always will. Victoria Park is a quiet spot in a noisy modern city and cannot be completely cut off from society's problems. Officials can only take so many precautions and then hope that troubles don't go beyond the level of tossing benches in the lake or tipping over garbage cans. The fault lies not in the nature of the park, but in the nature of humanity.

## "...POLISHING THE JEWEL..."

Following the 1894 ratepayers' vote to adopt the Public Parks Act, all Berlin parks were controlled by the Board of Park Management. At the time, there was only the Town Park (later named Woodside) followed shortly by Hibner Park, then Victoria Park. Six prominent men were selected by Town Council to sit for a three year term, with two members retiring each year. The mayor of the day was the board's seventh member. This structure, with little change, governed the community's parks until 1965. The Public Parks Act defined and limited funding to a maximum amount of 1/2 mill on the town's assessment. From this sum, and any dollars which came in from rentals and concession rights, the Park Board had to develop, maintain and improve the parks, pay wages, buy equipment, plants and insurance, plus cover all sundry expenses which occurred. Major land purchases and building construction were paid by debentures issued by Town Council. Often running for forty years, these debenture payments eventually strapped the board's ability to maintain the parks properly. In the early 1920s, the province relieved the pressure by increasing the allocation to one mill.

Following World War II, an organized recreation infrastructure grew rapidly in Kitchener. Since recreation and parks are closely allied, it was apparent by the mid 1960s that the two would work better as one. The Recreation Commission and Board of Park Management were dissolved. Those bodies re-emerged, via the province's 'City of Kitchener Act, 1965' as the Parks and Recreation Commission. On this body were eight council-appointed members plus the head of council and one other council member.

This combined commission oversaw the development of Kitchener's parks during rapid-growth years as the city spilled over its boundaries. Beginning with a lone park in 1894 Kitchener now had over thirty, of all shapes, sizes and uses. It was clear that professional management of such important resources was required. During the commission's tenure, trained parks and recreation administrators and planners such as Lloyd Minshall, Fred Graham, Tom Clancy, Bob Arnot, Harold Chase, Don McLaren and Bob Ballentyne appeared on staff.

When the city discontinued commission-style municipal operations in 1973, Parks and Recreation became a separate department of Kitchener City Council.

❦

The Park Board served Victoria Park's first 70 years well. A list of members is dotted with some of the community's most prominent names.

Grace Schmidt takes a back seat to no one in knowledge of local history. From the time she was born in 1915, Grace has observed and preserved the growth of Berlin/Kitchener. Still living in her family home just a block away, she savours many Victoria Park memories: school field days, skating and the caged animals. Grace particularly recalls the Zion Evangelical Church Sunday School picnics. A R Kaufman was a regular at these and

*"...he would come over to the playgrounds and catch us when we came down the slides."*

One image still clear in Grace's mind is of A R's mother, Mary, emerging from her son's chaffeur-driven automobile in the picnic grounds. First prize for most events was

*"...a pair of running shoes from the Kaufman Rubber Company."*

*Family names that span Berlin's existence and echo through the town's business life are found on this 1901 grouping of the Board of Park Management. At top, left to right, are August Lang, Karl Mueller, Louis J Breithaupt and on the bottom are George Rumpel, William Roos and J S Hoffman.*

Of the initial six, August Lang, William Roos, J S Hoffman, Thomas Bridger, C F Brown, and L J Breithaupt, Roos served until 1911, Breithaupt until 1909. Daniel Hibner, mayor in 1894, was appointed a member in 1909, became chairman and remained until 1918.

One remarkable Park Board member, indeed one of the city's most remarkable men, joined in 1924 and was still there at amalgamation with recreation 41 years later. Known most commonly by his initials, A R Kaufman never held elected office but worked on numerous committees, commissions and boards. A R gave not only of his time and effort but used his wealth to increase and improve Kitchener's parks. The swimming pool is at Woodside Park because of a Kaufman gift. Kaufman Park is named after him and was also made possible by his land donation. Several north ward parks have Kaufman roots. That A R also chaired the Kitchener Planning Commission (later Board) through much of his Park Board tenure helped co-ordinate plans of these two bodies.

Oscar Lauber joined the board in 1931, became chairman within two years and remained a member until 1957, making a formidable pairing with A R Kaufman.

Ellroy Lippert was a second-generation Park Board member serving from

1940 until 1957 at which time he became Parks Administrator. His father, George, sat on the board before World War I.

Several prominent appointees were Victoria Park neighbours. Homer Ford, member and chairman in the 1916-24 period, built and lived in a beautiful two-fronted house at the corner of Heins and Water South. D Alex Bean, 1921-27 member and chairman, enjoyed a lovely view of the park from his Roland Street home. Both Lipperts' homes overlooked Victoria Park, one from Heins, one from Roland. J M Staebler, a member and chairman from early 1896 to 1898, had a most beautiful view of the early park from 'Buena Vista', his home at 379 Queen South. J M's son, H L Staebler sat 13 years on the board beginning in 1936. W H E Schmalz lived at the corner of Courtland and Queen so had a one-block-removed interest during his 1936-56 period as a Park Board member.Two-time chairman Karl Mueller kept an eye on the park from his Roland Street home.

❧

In the days of a small number of parks, few permanent employees and a limited budget, the board style of management worked well. But Kitchener was growing and its park and recreation functions grew. With full-time professional management replacing the board system in the 1960s and 70s longer-term planning and budgeting were possible to meet the public demand for a rapidly expanding network of services. Today, Victoria Park is just one of 170 parks in Kitchener, totalling over 3,000 acres. These are classified in five categories: neighbourhood, community, district, city and regional. Officially Victoria Park comes under the middle three in that list but an argument could easily be made that it fits all five. As such an important member of that 170 total, Victoria Park receives Parks and Recreation's highest standard of maintenance and upkeep, with the most attention of any park.

Tom Clancy, the city's general manager of Parks and Recreation, proudly calls Victoria "our major downtown jewel...the heart of Kitchener's extensive open space system for all our citizens."

# VICTORIA PARK...
# AN ALBUM

An eight-columned pergola stood on the Roland shore from 1922 until the mid 1930s. It proved to be a popular snapshot site. Dorothy Russell and Faith White stopped by the pristine structure in 1924. By the '30s it had started to deteriorate. The four Gofton girls were well-known around Victoria Park in the late 1920s and early 1930s. From their home at 117 David Street the pergola was just a short stroll away for Jerene, Annette, Eleanor and Marion Gofton.

The Heins pergola also appeared in 1922, originally boasting attractive latticed sides. This unknown trio, posing in the mid 1930s, appears on a series of Victoria Park snapshots recently discovered in an area antique store.

At the urging of the Ontario Motor League, Kitchener Park Board set aside a small area at the park's southwestern end for touring motorists. In the '30s visitors were charged 50¢ a day including two free showers in the nearby tourist kitchen shelter. Opened in 1923, the tourist camp shut down in 1968 when the park's ring road was closed.

Victoria Park's first playground was set up in 1911 between the poplar row and the railway tracks near Devon Street. Called 'Frolic Park' its crude equipment was soon relocated to a site near the pavilion. In 1914, Dorothy Russell (standing on swing), her aunt Florence Schantz (left), grandmother Mary Moyer Schantz (standing) and friends enjoyed a swing ride. The $350 'Pony-Cycle' merry-go-round was a popular addition in 1947. This group can't wait for the Record's photographer to finish so they can set it spinning again.

Playground safety standards have tightened markedly over the past 20 years and equipment design reflects this new emphasis. Over the winter of 1995-96 an innovative, fully accessible play facility began replacing the set-up shown here. Only the "twirley slide" remains from this early 1995 playground scene.

Bring the kids to Victoria Park! Sharron and Sandra Mills set their sights on having winter fun in 1951. A year before that, Patsy Farrow got all the excitement she needed in the baby swing. The author of this book was paddled around the lake in 1950 by his uncle, Bruce Gress. Below, Martha Snyder and her mother, Priscilla, enjoy a drink in 1907 from an early park water tap. Shirley Egerdeen visited the park in 1954 for one reason — the best ice surface in the area. Exuberance flows from a mid 1920s shot of Velma and Ernie Russell near the bandstand.

VICTORIA PARK
RAIN CHECK
KITCHENER PANTHERS

How different the game was at the turn-of-the-century! No gloves, only 9 players dressed, mandatory facial hair and diamond-pattern socks. The Berlin Maple Leafs Base Ball Club prepares for action in front of the original grandstand. On May 19, 1919, professional baseball came to Kitchener and Mayor David Gross (right) headed the civic delegation welcoming the Michigan Ontario League. The Kitchener Beavers and Battle Creek Custers lined up before the game which Kitchener won 2-1. The houses in the background, above the Beavers, are on Water Street.

An exciting 1947 playoff game between Kitchener Panthers and London Majors of the Inter County Senior League featured a run down between home and third. London batter Don Cooper watches as team-mate Gord McMahon tries to avoid a tag. Panther pitcher Bobby Schnurr covers home plate for catcher Harry Psutka. Third baseman Roy Musselman is about to throw the ball while shortstop Bobby Fischer backs him up. Umpire Mickey McDonald oversees the action. Note the overflow crowd sitting along and on top of the outfield fence. Roy Musselman loaned this photo, a treasured memento for him from almost 50 years ago.

70

In July 1955, Kitchener's first (and only?) incident of flagpole sitting took place. Panthers' reserve pitcher Jerry Fryfogel was unhappy with fan support and vowed to live on top of a Victoria Park flagpole until 2,000 people passed through the turnstiles. Suffering from stomach disorders after seven days in thunderstorms and intense heat, Fryfogel was taken down by the Kitchener Fire Department.

Association football, now known as soccer, was "the only game that moved the Berliners to cheer" in the 1880s, according to W V Uttley. The sport came to Berlin when David Forsyth introduced it to his high school students in the late 1870s. His collegiate teams won several titles as did a town club, also organized by Forsyth, called the Rangers. The 1890s team photo taken with David Street in the background shows Forsyth seated at left and George DeBus at right with cane. The 1924 edition of the Rangers also posed in Victoria Park. Listed on the original matte are: (back row) G Hanna, J Turner, C Hodgson, J. Richardson (Pres.), A Ashcroft, C Nispel (Capt.), J McColl, J Whitle, H Ballantyne (Mgr.), W Gardner, E Chapman, J Blake (Sec.); (front row) E Hill, W Barnes, J Wey, B Burnham, T Langon.

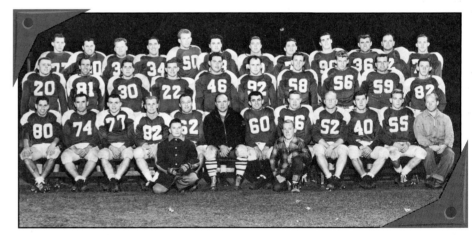

The Ontario Rugby Football Union had a solid entry in Kitchener and the pigskin heyday was the mid 1950s when the Dutchmen hosted Balmy Beach Bombers, Sarnia Imperials and London Lords. In October 1953 action between Balmy Beach and the Dutchmen, the ball carrier seems destined to be tackled. Portable bleachers in the background have been moved out from their usual baseball location behind the right field fence. The Dutchmen's annual team picture in 1955 was a night shot.

Starting in 1895 with Richard Cowan, caretaker of Berlin's 'New Park', and Fritz Kruse, appointed in 1896 to supervise Victoria Park, hundreds and hundreds of men and women have worked in the park. Let the ten on this page represent those hundreds. On a sunny winter's afternoon in the early 1940s four workers pause for a photo: Harry Gofton, Bill McCarley, George 'Scotty' Fraser and Frank 'Franz' Rabethge.

A park employee from 1930 until 1958, Rabethge is shown again with the newest lawn mower. Compare that 1948 machine with the model Barney Zarzycki was riding just eight years later. Youngsters eagerly awaited the hanging of the swings each spring. On a bright May 1952 day, Bill Wojnowski installs the baby swings. An attractive 1959 addition to Victoria Park was the model lighthouse in a small pool near the Water Street entrance. Building it are Ken Shiry and Henry Eckert, each of whom spent over 35 years on staff before retiring in the 1990s.

At the 1924 Courtland entrance gates, gardener Teresa Hargreaves and Tammy Bender prepare the flowerbeds for the 1996 season.

72

Luella and Nelda Shelley of Conestogo moved to Kitchener in the early 1920s to find work. They often strolled through Victoria Park where one sister photographed the other on Roos Island in 1922. Another island photo taken 15 years later also focuses more on flowers than people. Victoria Park gardener Matt Potje brought his family to the island to enjoy the tulip blossoms. On the bench, behind the flowerbed, are sons Johnny, Matt Jr, Joe, neighbour Mrs Punhoffer and Johanna Potje. In 1956, Matt Potje is nearing retirement age but the pansy beds get careful attention from the head gardener and a Victoria Park pal.

The Water Street raised flowerbed always attracted admiring onlookers with its innovativ designs. The 1963 version honoured the American satellite Faith Seven. The living plant representing the satellite were supported in mid-air. In more recent years, the Roland bed has been eagerly awaited by neighbours to see what colourful patterns will emer Parks and Recreation staff's imaginations.

Victoria Park was only a couple of years old when floods began plaguing the neighbourhood. The original floodgates, even when extensively modified, could not handle sudden, heavy downpours. A 1922 flood photo, looking up David Street from Hilda Place, also provides a good view of the first boathouse. The August 1968 view from an airplane was all too familiar to residents who came to expect annual deluges. The floodgate itself has almost disappeared and the land behind David Street is under water. Following complete floodgate and lake outlet reconstruction in 1984-85, some problems did still crop up. A heavy rainstorm in July 1991 clogged the outlet and the backed-up waters submerged even the boathouse dock. That 1985 construction installed massive storm sewer tiles under the lake. They carry runoff from the downtown area into Schneider Creek beyond the floodgates. Periodic dredging of accumulated silt is still necessary. A major project in early winter 1994 removed almost two meters of muck which had washed into the lake since the 1985 construction.

The first building erected in Victoria Park was a boathouse and there's been one ever since. Visitors could rent a canoe or rowboat as most of these people have done, or could bring their own. That's what Dorothy Russell (above) did in this 1922 scene in the north channel. The David Street boathouse is seen below in a long shot from the Roland bridge. Its replacement was built in 1929.

When Nick Ozaruk, George Moskal and Ralph Sutton wanted a boys' day out in the early 1940s they rented a canoe from the second boathouse. The Roland bridge arches over Helga Hartman as her companion snaps a 1958 shot. In the main picture, taken around 1912, the busy-ness of a Berlin afternoon in Victoria Park comes across clearly. Everyone's wearing Sunday best although one canoeist has taken his jacket off to make paddling a little more comfortable. The photographer faces northeast from the present location of the fountain bridge.

A good place to be with friends — that's Victoria Park! Young and old, serious and playful. In January 1923, two of Dorothy Russell's friends visited Kitchener. Verna Fraser and Helen Lockie enjoyed a winter day's tour of the park and stopped for a snapshot on Roos Island with Dorothy (centre). Monument bases make good photo spots and in 1933 Carly and Marietta Gibbons paused beneath Queen Victoria with their son. In 1913, Mary Moyer Schantz brought a friend to the park for a stroll. As they were taking a break on the Peace Memorial base, Dorothy Russell took a snapshot of her grandmother (left) and friend.

In the spring of 1950, Edeltraut and Gustav Petsche had just met and their first date was in Victoria Park. Gustav set the timer on the camera, dashed to the bench, put his arm around Edeltraut and they've been together ever since. Thirty-eight years later Anita Petsche and Paul Good chose Victoria Park for their wedding photo session on May 14, 1988.

Kitchener City Hall, seen here in the 1920s, was designed by W H E Schmalz and B A Jones. It stood from 1924 to 1973 when a controversial decision was made to demolish it and sell the land. Fortunately, the prominent clock tower and century-old bell, aptly named Victoria, were preserved. For 20 years the stone pieces lay in various sites including a Chandler Drive field. Several projects were brought up suggesting the tower's reconstruction but all died in the planning stages. Then Dean Zinken came on the scene. Quietly he rallied support to rebuild the tower as a heritage structure in Victoria Park. The general manager of Parks and Recreation, Tom Clancy, was another long-time supporter but the $400,000 cost was always the stumbling block. In December 1994 a unique proposal came from the Waterloo, Wellington, Dufferin and Grey Building and Construction Trades Council. Along with Conestoga College they initiated a job training program that attracted federal retraining funds. The March 17, 1995 ground-breaking ceremony preceded three months of hectic volunteer work by business, labour, the municipality and educational institutions. Mayor Richard Christy and Herb Schmalz (son of the architect) triggered the clock mechanism into action on July 1. When Victoria Park's 100th Birthday celebrations began on New Year's Eve, activities centred around the park's newest attraction. Musicians, singers and the Free Flow Dance Company entertained a large crowd and everyone counted down to 1996.

A St Andrew's Presbyterian Church picnic is about to begin in Victoria Park. Fourth from left, in white, is Sophie Cleghorn, wife of W G Cleghorn. Her granddaughter, Margaret Farrow, has loaned her collection of family photographs to the Victoria Park archives. Family reunions in Victoria Park were a regular occurrence in the early days. A 1913 get-together brought members of the Schantz-Moyer clan to Berlin. Dorothy Russell, whose mother had been a Schantz, is second girl from left in front. In the background is Schneider Island.

To open the Joseph Schneider Haus 1996 exhibition featuring Victoria Park artifacts, memorabilia and photographs, Queen Victoria came out of retirement again. Members of the Victoria Park 100th Birthday Historical Committee in this February 1996 photo are Johanna Jamnik, Miriam Sokvitne, Lorna Ferguson, Dorothy Russell, Mark Yantzi and Glennis Yantzi. The exhibit, A Century of Rest and Recreation, ran from February 19 to August 25, 1996.

A bird's-eye view in May 1916 from the top of the Arrow Shirt factory on Benton Street. The poplar row stands out as do seven identical homes on Henry Street. The 1919 aerial view, the first-known of the park, positions Schneider Avenue at the bottom and Heins Avenue angling down brightly from the top. The dark scar at bottom left is the site of the original pavilion, at this time completely cleared away.

The August 1965 overhead photo outlines how Park Street split in two directions. A right turn took one over the concrete bridge, through the picnic grounds and connected with a tree-fringed Schneider Avenue. Several sets of railway tracks snaked around the western edge of Victoria Park. The old Preston and Berlin Electric Railway, later known as the Grand River Railway, crossed both Park and Theresa before heading up to Joseph Street. The twin set of spurs at extreme right led to shipping sheds behind William Knell and Company on Victoria Street South. All three pair of tracks were washed out in the late 1980s by severe storms. In 1996 only the Galt Branch of the CNR remains in operation.

David Schneider was born in 1840 and grew up on the land that became Victoria Park. Later in life he lived on Schneider Avenue and on Dill Street and was a familiar figure in the park. During a stroll in the early 1900s he's photographed near Schneider Island. Dorothy Russell (right) and Frank Schantz prepare for a tennis match in 1925. Several courts were installed and maintained by the Park Board in the 1910-1930 period. Some were located beside the Queen Victoria monument and others, such as this one, on the south shore near the pavilion. Dorothy was one of the annual renters, paying $12 for a season's use.

How many differences can you spot between this clever, late 1920s shot of the bridge and bandstand, and the same scene today? On Roos Island, a new event in the 1990s brought mediaeval warriors out in force. 'Ye Old Annualle Victoriae Parke Islandie Fayrie' recreated customs and skills from the Middle Ages utilizing members of the Society for Creative Anachronism.

# "...THE FUTURE COMES BACK..."

*envisioned by Dan Daly, Leslie Bamford and Tom Clancy*
*Kitchener Parks and Recreation*

Now, the year is 2096. Some things never change: Victoria Park continues to be regularly enjoyed by citizens of Kitchener as a haven from the pressures of their busy lifestyles and as a place to connect with nature and history.

In the past 100 years, Kitchener has grown substantially. Traffic volume is a burning issue so efficient public transit is in place. Gas-combustion vehicles no longer exist: engines are run by hydrogen. People rarely drive personal units into the downtown core as parking fees are prohibitive. Public transit is most efficient: at each stop's voice-box people can order a unit to be routed their way immediately. Computerized routing ensures that people are moved expeditiously.

The main public transit line runs from Cambridge on the old rail line corridor to Kitchener where it passes beside Victoria Park on its way to Metropolitan St Jacobs which is now Kitchener's Twin City. Most visitors to Victoria Park use public transit. The old parking lots have been turned into grassy nooks interspersed with flower beds, fountains and benches. Fitness-oriented visitors still walk from nearby neighbourhoods or use bicycles which they leave at glassed-in, secure kiosks covered by vines. Some visitors fly in: personal forms of air transportation may land at the park's aeropads. Ultra-lite planes aren't uncommon, being popular and affordable, although the in-vogue battery-run helicopters are still somewhat rare and expensive.

'Old City Hall', built long ago in 1993, marks the start of the visitor's stroll down the soft Pedestrian Mall on Gaukel Street, leading to Victoria Park. Cafes and specialty shops line the route, many selling low-fat, nutritious and vegetarian snacks to the health-oriented population. A large greensward welcomes you to the park, inviting all to walk, play and enjoy relief from the rigors of noisy city life. The 170 year old historic Clock Tower at the park's entrance calls out a greeting to all, carolling melodies over the open commons. Victoria Park is a haven of peace and serenity.

Park lawns are lush and manicured, a major attraction since green spaces in Kitchener are limited. Only a few private golf courses boast grass of similar quality. Meadow grass in Victoria Park grows 10.2 centimetres long and is delightful to walk on. Shiny, deep green blades attract the eye while the soft springy texture attracts the feet, daring people to go barefoot or even lie down to read, chat or daydream.

Irrigation and fertilization are controlled automatically through underground piping monitored by computerized sensors. Integrated pest management operates similarly. Sensors monitoring rain, sun, temperature, and humidity calculate which treatments are required then apply systemic sprays underground which are absorbed through plant roots. Ants, for instance, have been eliminated from the picnic area through use of this system. Picnics are much more pleasant than in the 'olden days.'

Annuals grace geometric beds in delightful patterns. Many trees are huge, some nearly 200 years old. Each tree is marked with a bronze plaque indicating type and year planted. The variety is unmatched, making this a popular spot for those interested in forestry or birds. Few nesting sites are left anywhere else in the city so the many birdhouses abounding in the park and the computerized birdseed distributors attract those species which survived the great mid-century die-off. Dog owners also love the park. A large area of dog runs controlled by invisible computer-operated fences, is open throughout the day. Dogs can be exercised with no danger of fights or attacks since the dog is unable to escape its own control area. Computer-operated cleaning techniques electrolysize droppings and transform them into odour-free fertilizer which is added to the park's flowerbeds.

The lake: pure and blue! A pair of Royal Mute swans dips and glides along the azure ripples. Storm water is strictly controlled, entering in clean, limited volumes having been purified through ground-water recharging. Lake water is continuously oxygenated by wind-driven aerators. In winter, Kitchener-developed outdoor climate control techniques produce perfect ice surfaces for the maximum skating period.

Victoria Park is home to many art forms. Bridges, pagodas, bandshells, pergolas and monuments are decorated with a variety of sculptures, etchings and carvings in bronze, wood, cement and milclan, all detailing local history and culture.

One hundred thousand attend the 200th Anniversary Week in the park. Large musical productions, special light-speed effects shows, outdoor plays, multicultural ceremonies, air shows and local town fayres entertain everyone. There's even a round-the-lake race with participants all over 100 years of age.

Fitness-walking trails, some 300 miles of which snake through the Twin Cities, converge on the park. Trails are dotted by monitoring stations which keep individual statistics on pace, calorie-burn, past performance and suggested intake proportions.

Yes, 2096. Thanks to people such as Daniel Hibner and William Roos and L J Breithaupt back in 1896, we have a Victoria Park. Nowadays it's more important to Kitchener citizens than ever. We look back at the outdated lake dredgings, the concerns about the Clock Tower reconstruction, the fight for community playgrounds and how they celebrated the 100th anniversary and understand how all this led to so many new opportunities. We're glad they fought it through.

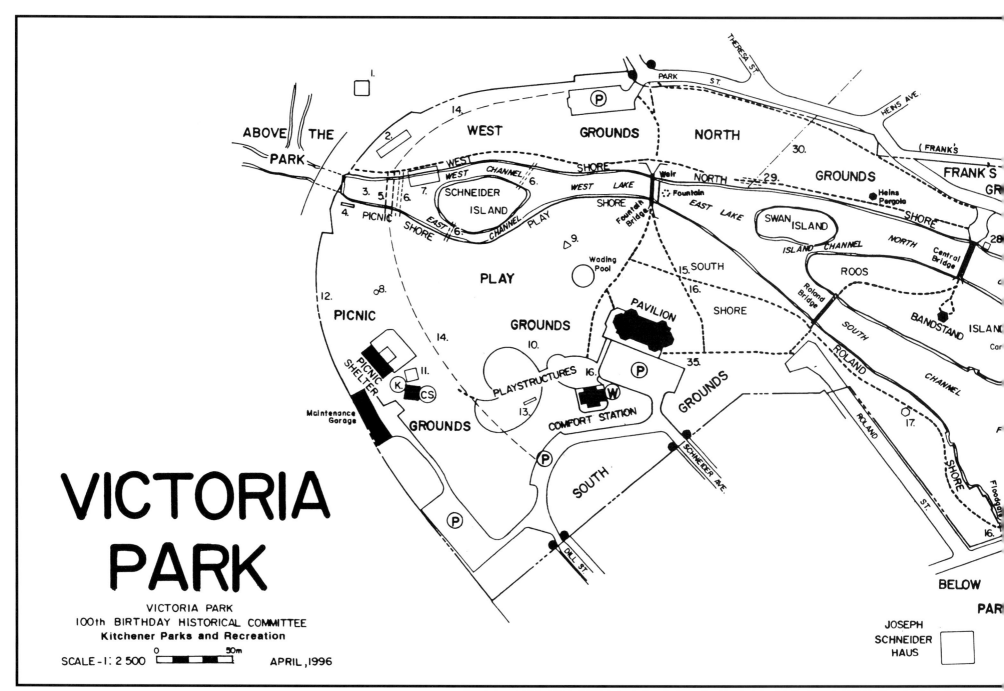

# VICTORIA PARK

VICTORIA PARK
100th BIRTHDAY HISTORICAL COMMITTEE
**Kitchener Parks and Recreation**

SCALE -1: 2 500    APRIL,1996

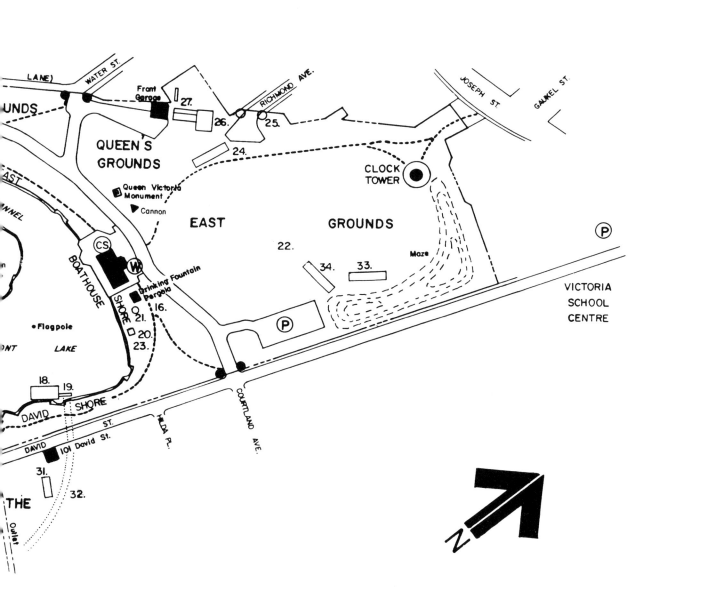

## HISTORICAL POINTS OF INTEREST

1. Old Glue Factory Chimney
2. Old Fowl & Animal Enclosure
3. Old Swimming Hole
4. Old Change House
5. Old Concrete Bridge
6. Old Wood Bridge
7. Old Beaver & Bear Pen
8. Old Drinking Fountain
9. Old W.W. I Cannon
10. Old Deer Run Area
11. Old Tourist Kitchen
12. Old Tourist Camp
13. Old Animal Cages
14. Old Roadway Until 1968
15. Monument
16. Plaque
17. Old Pergola
18. Old Boathouse
19. Old Floodgate
20. Peace Memorial & Kaiser Wilhelm I Bust
21. Old Mineral Water Well
22. Old Athletic Park & Grounds
23. Grandstand - 188? to 1895
24. Grandstand - 1896 to 1912
25. Old Entrance Gates
26. Old Park Superintendent Residence
27. Old Greenhouses
28. Old Booth
29. Old Rustic Bridge
30. Old Victoria St. Storm Drain
31. Old Icehouse
32. Old Lake Outlet
33. Grandstand - 1912 to 1919
34. Grandstand - 1919 to 1966
35. Geodetic Monument

### LEGEND

(CS) - Concession Stand

(P) - Parking

(W) - Washrooms

● ● Entrance Gate

------ Pathway

(K) - Picnic Summer Kitchen

mp.

83

# Footnotes Explanation

Event facts are often sourced in the text, and where not, have been taken from the next day's newspaper coverage or the Park Board Minutes of that month. Quotes and amplification of events have been footnoted. Since there has been so much erroneous information published on Victoria Park, I have felt free to point out these stumbling blocks in the footnotes. Comments on these writings and other opinions expressed in the footnotes are solely those of the author, rych mills.

Abbreviations.

| | |
|---|---|
| Record | The newspaper known variously as Berlin Daily Record, Berlin News (-) Record, The News Record,The Daily Record, Kitchener Daily Record, Kitchener Record, Kitchener-Waterloo Record, and the Record during the period studied here (1893 - 1996 ). |
| Telegraph | The Daily Telegraph newspaper, 1895 - 1922. (absorbed by the Record in 1922). |
| PB Minutes | The Berlin/Kitchener Board of Park Management minutes books are on file at the clerk's office in Kitchener City Hall. |
| VPHC | Victoria Park Historical Committee began in 1991 to research this publication. A photo and information archive was created. Ultimate destination of the archives is KPL. |
| WHSR | The annual report of the Waterloo Historical Society. |
| KPL | The Grace Schmidt Room at Kitchener Public Library contains the local history collection of the library,plus the Waterloo Historical Society's archives and a wealth of other collections. Microfilm copies of newspapers quoted in this book were those in the GSR's collection. |
| KPRCD | Kitchener Parks and Recreation on Chandler Drive has a valuable historical collection of documents from the 1890s on. |
| KPRCH | Kitchener Parks and Recreation at City Hall has a collection of more recent documents and photographs. |
| CGC | Conrad Grebel College at the University of Waterloo, Waterloo, contains among others, the Joseph Meyer Snyder Family Fonds, a substantial collection of Schneider/Snyder documentation. The Gordon Eby Collection was also found valuable. |
| UWSCL | The Special Collections Library at the University of Waterloo Library contains the Historical Photographic Negative collection of the Record. The Breithaupt-Hewetson-Clark collection details the vibrant life of the Breithaupt family in this community and it is located in the Special Collections Library. |
| JSHM | Joseph Schneider Haus Museum located beside Victoria Park maintains the Schneider homestead in its 19th century form. There is a valuable archive of material and artefacts. |
| Rec Photo | The Record maintains an historical photograph archive at its Fairway Road location. Although there is no set timeframe it would seem to contain pre 1940 material mainly. Photographs after that date, as well as some before, are at UWSCL. |

1) Galen Cranz. *The Politics of Park Design*. Cambridge, Mass.: 1982. p10

2) Bruce Trigger. *The Children of Aataentsic I*. Montreal: 1976. p95

3) David Boyle. *Archaeological Report 1894-95*. Toronto: 1896. p34

4) Bruce Trigger. *Natives and Newcomers: Canada's "Heroic Age" Reconsidered*. Kingston and Montreal : McGill and Queens University Press, 1985. pp235, 260, 271, 288

5) The Mississauga name for the Grand River was Pesshineguning Oeskinneguning: 'the one that washes the timber down and drives away grass weeds.' From E Reginald Good's original draft of 'Mississauga-Mennonite Relations In The Upper Grand River Valley' Ontario History, June 1995 quoting Augustus Jones' Surveyor's Letters, July 4 1796 in the Provincial Archives of Ontario. I have been unable to trace any Mississauga name for Schneider Creek. Elizabeth Bloomfield, in her massive study, *Waterloo Township Through Two Centuries* p26 notes it was once called Beasley's Creek. The name appears on a very early map but there seems to be no other such Beasley reference. Either it had minimal usage, was a map-maker's invention or was an error. Naming the stream after the Schneiders probably came simply from use. Neatly bisecting Lot 17, the major stream in the area would easily have taken on the owner's name.

6) Good, 'Mississauga-Mennonite Relations in the Upper Grand River Valley' p169. An earlier draft of this published article titled 'Colonizing a People' goes into more detail. There is a copy in VPHC.

7) quoted in Good, p169. Good quotes Donald Smith, *Sacred Feathers* p223. Smith mentions it came from a news clipping of August 15, 1845.

8) Donald Smith, 'Maungwudas Goes Abroad', in *Beaver Magazine,* Autumn 1976. p4

9) Good, p167

10) Smith, 'Maungwudas Goes Abroad'p6, and Good, 'Mississauga-Mennonite Relations.' p167

11) W V Uttley, 'Joseph Schneider: Founder of the City,' WHSR 1929.Waterloo: 1930. p116

12) I am grateful to Reg Good and Sandra Woolfrey for guiding me through the imprecise world of Aboriginal and native history of Waterloo Township and Southern Ontario. Until recently, history ( i.e. white man's history) has skimmed over the vibrant life of this land before 1800. The subtle (and at times, overt) racism of both popular and academic history has of late been undergoing long overdue reconsideration. Reg's study from the June 1995 Ontario History (available at KPL) is particularly pertinent to any Kitchener story.

13) Ezra Eby. *A Biographical History of Waterloo Township*. Kitchener: E D Weber, 1971. p18

14) (Joseph M Snyder) *Hannes Schneider*. pp112, 150A

15)– *Assessment For the Township of Waterloo for 1816*. The Archives of Ontario, Toronto. This document dates the current Joseph Schneider Haus to at least four years earlier than the previously accepted 1820.

16) (Joseph M Snyder) *Hannes Schneider*. p128A
17) (Joseph M Snyder) *Hannes Schneider*. pp116, 117

18)– *Map of Part of the Town of Berlin, capital of the County of Waterloo C.W.,* surveyed for George John Grange, Esq by M C Schofield P L S. 1853-54. Note, at this time Berlin had just been given status as an incorporated village. Not until 1870-71 was Berlin officially a town. Cityhood came in 1912. For Varnum reference, see KPL's Varnum family vertical file for correspondence on subject of which Varnum first approached Joseph Schneider...Phineas or Prescott.

19)(Joseph M Snyder) *Hannes Schneider*. p115

20) Victoria Park Myth. Beginning in 1954 with the city's centennial booklet and the June 22 Record centennial souvenir (possibly researched by the same person) numerous articles have focused on the catchy headline: 'Victoria Park Once Criticized For Being Too Far Out!' This is nonsense. In 1894, the criticism 'Too Far Out' was aimed at the Town Park (Woodside). Those who favoured a new park (Victoria) said the Town Park was too far from downtown. Those 1954 researchers perhaps didn't realize there was a Town Park before Victoria.

21) Uttley, *History of Kitchener*. p283. Uttley's book is fascinating but frustrating. Few sources are given for the wealth of information it contains; thus it must be treated with caution. A 1975 reissue by Wilfrid Laurier University Press contains biographical information on Uttley, an introduction by Gerald Noonan and a welcome index.

22) The introduction of this tidy little photograph souvenir booklet not only caused a ruckus in 1901 as outlined in the captions, but kept Staebler's supposedly-prominent role alive for decades. In *The Province of Ontario* this introduction is printed verbatim. Daniel Hibner, in a reflective article in the Record of March 13, 1920, also gives a great deal of credit to Staebler for originating the new park idea. The PB Minutes of July 27, 1901 mention that Staebler 'edited' the booklet. Editing could include writing. Also see a series of letters to the Record July 22, 27, 31 of 1901.

23) Record, October 30, 1894. Too much credit has been given to Ricker in the designing of Victoria Park. In effect he simply confirmed what Bowman and Hartmuth had produced. His visit cost the Park Board $33.40.

24) For Hibner's view of the park's origins see Record, March 13, 1920 and *The Province of Ontario*. Each of these however contains the erroneous information from the 1901 Staebler booklet introduction.

25) Brown's offer-to-buy on December 2, 1895 was not followed up by the Park Board. Both it and its chairman, after reflection, realized his action although dramatic, had been unwise. The letter attached to his cheque had ended: "Your Much Abused Chairman of the Board of Park Management.' Tragically, Brown was dead within nine weeks. Blood poisoning had sapped the life of the 51 year old energetic entrepreneur. Replacing him on the Park Board, and in the chair, was J M Staebler.

26) Record, March 10, 1938. Anonymous charcoal sketch done from a family photograph portrait taken around 1880. Loaned by Evelyn and Arthur Hewitt, grandchildren of William.

27) Telegraph, January 12, 1916. In a front page editorial the Telegraph's D Alex Bean attacked the Park Board and its chairman Daniel Hibner for their reluctance to spend money on ice cleaning and grooming for outdoor skating in Victoria Park. After shepherding the argument neatly, Bean buries the rapier. Citizens would be wise to '...bear the fact in mind that he (Hibner) is President of the Berlin Auditorium Company.' Of course the auditorium (on Queen South where Charles now intersects) offered revenue-generating *indoor* skating.

28) Record, August 14, 1896.

29) KPRCD

30) Returnees to the city continued to be amazed by the transformation. The April 11, 1929 Record interviews Alexander Gibson visiting his sister, Mrs Charles Pirie of 37 Roland Street. Gibson starred on the 1888 champion Berlin Rangers soccer club, then left town for the USA. He stared unbelievingly at the beautiful park vistas where his memory could only recall Samuel Schneider farming.

31) Karl Mueller. *'Onkel Karl'*. Bremen: 1924. Karl Mueller was Park Board chairman in 1901-03 and again in 1909. He then returned to live in Germany but apparently kept in touch with Berlin, Ontario. His memoirs of life in Canada were published in Bremen, Germany in 1924. Joseph M Snyder reprinted the chapter titled 'Onkel Karl' in *Hannes Schneider*. Translation by Geertje Gubitz is at VPHC. Mueller died in August 1929 in Germany.

32) KPRCD has a copy of the agreement dated November 11, 1895. Another of those Victoria Park Myths says these guns were captured in the Crimean War. There is no evidence. They are standard British ordnance pieces.

33) Record, January 18, 1919.

34) Record, October 22, 1940.

35) Record, May 11, 1992. John Kiely's column quotes the author and others but claims both cannon were once on the island. I find nothing to confirm this.

36) Record, September 22, 1896. The Record castigates the Telegraph. Unfortunately the Telegraph is missing for this month from the KPL collection. This is a good place to alert the reader. Two things should be kept in mind when considering the Peace Memorial and Kaiser's bust. The monument honoured the Friedensfest of 1871 in Berlin, Ontario. The bust was of Kaiser Wilhelm I, dead in 1888. His grandson Wilhelm II was the German leader in World War I. Some observers, looking back carelessly, mistakenly assume the bust was of the 'enemy' leader during the war, thus allowing a certain amount of sympathy to be extended to the bust-topplers.

37) Record, September 22, 1896. The list totals $674.50 and contains over 70 names, almost all from Berlin. For Seagram's contribution, see Record, January 15, 1897.

38) Record, August 13, 1897. The Record's very extensive coverage appeared on the day of the unveiling. Again, the Telegraph of this period is not on microfilm at KPL.

39) L J Breithaupt, Diaries, August 1897. In the Breithaupt-Hewetson-Clark Collection, UWSCL. That this event meant a lot to Louis J is evident in the amount of feeling he puts into his usually straightforward diary entries.

40) Record, August 13, 1897. All quotes from this date. A little genealogy here might help. Wilhelm II was the son of Frederick, Crown Prince of Prussia (later Kaiser of Germany) and Victoria, Princess Royal, eldest daughter of Queen Victoria. Wilhelm II became German Kaiser in 1888, abdicated in November 1918 and lived in exile in Holland until his death in 1941. A S Nordhimer is elsewhere spelt Nordheimer.

41) Evelyn Hahn of Kitchener has identified the two boys in striped suits as her father Gordon Maier and his brother Clayton. They lived at 26 Courtland West. The Knechtel boys' home was 31 Courtland West. Mrs Patricia (Knechtel) Perrett has identified her father Carl and uncle Otto as well as the Maier boys. Harvey Grasser's name is in Carl's handwriting on a copy of this photo in her possession. Grasser was on the police force from 1909 until 1950, serving as chief for two years before retirement. However, his son Ted Grasser says the large man in the photo is not his father, Harvey. Newspaper reports of the day mention constable Meehan being involved in the search, so perhaps he is the unidentified figure.

42) Telegraph, August 31, 1905. Prince Louis was father of Louis, Earl Mountbatten of Burma, 1900 - 1979.

43) Probably the most-studied period in the community's history. See day-by-day coverage in the newspapers of the time. Numerous articles from later years, academic studies, theses, school reports and oral history remembrances are on file at KPL. Published studies of varying depth and dependability include: John English and Kenneth McLaughlin, *Kitchener: An Illustrated History*; Gottlieb Leibbrandt, *Little Paradise*; Patricia McKegney, *The Kaiser's Bust*; Bill Moyer, *Kitchener: Yesterday Revisited* and W R Chadwick, *The Battle For Berlin: An Historical Drama*. On September 1, 1916 Berlin became Kitchener.

44) Record, September 20, 1956; October 4, 1966 as noted in text. In addition to the melt-down theory, other accounts have the bust buried in a downtown backyard; kept in a wood shed on a nearby farm; secreted away by a cabal within the Concordia Club (successor to the Concordia Society); thrown back in the lake and lost in the mud; or kept for 20 years by a small group then melted down in the mid 30s when the rise of Naziism threatened further tensions in Kitchener. See January 1995 issue of *Spoke*, the Conestoga College student newspaper. An article by Patricia Bow outlines recent studies. As the 80th anniversary of the bust's disappearance approached, the Record February 13, 1996, ran a front page story. A number of calls provided new leads, more myths, guesses and theories. It also resulted in the re-discovery of the whereabouts of the Bismarck medallion and a second napkin ring. Both are in a private collector's possession in Toronto.

45) Gordon Eby's daughter, Anne Millar, still has some of his photographs including this view of the Queen's statue. There is no mention in his diaries of attending a ceremony at the monument.

46) KPL. Minutes, scrapbooks, and memorabilia of the Princess of Wales Chapter of the IODE were recently donated to the Grace Schmidt Room at KPL. Much information from these records was used in this chapter.

47) Telegraph, March 25, 1909.

48) Record, August 18, 1910. The Record quotes an article in the '...leading Roman daily, the Corrierre D'Italia....' I have followed the Italian newspaper's spelling of Zaccaquini's name. There are several variants in Berlin references of the period. The Funcken statue was recently moved from the closed St Jerome's High School property on Duke Street to the Young Street lawn of St Mary's Roman Catholic Church.

49) Telegraph, May 29 and 30, 1911. Very extensive coverage of the event with complete texts of all the speeches.

50) Record, March 21, 1914.

51) J M Nyce, editor, *The Gordon Eby Diaries* pp79,81. Among the many activities he enjoys in Victoria Park, Eby mentions ball games, reunions, skating and boating.

52) Telegraph, July 5, 1907. Mackenzie King attended many rallies, receptions and picnics in Victoria Park. His boyhood home, Woodside, is a National Historic Site and Park on Wellington Street North. It should not be confused with Woodside Park on Queen Street South.

53) Record, June 10, 1915.

54) Telegraph, June 17, 1910. Fines ranged from $10 to $20.

55) PB Minutes, July 15, 1954. Also see May 19, 1933.

56) Record, September 20, 1920. The un-named Park Board member gave no reasons for his suggestion.

57) Record, May 25, 1912 for abolishing Park Board. The wording in this paragraph ('...meetings, decisions, committees, arguments, decisions, reverses, decisions, legal wrangles...') is not meant to mislead. The 1910-12 period is a mind-numbing experience if one tries to follow all the ins-and-outs as the board, the town, the province and many organizations clashed over plans to alter the athletic grounds. Some subsequent writers on the park have become lost in the maze. See Bill Moyer, Yesterday Revisited excerpt in K-W Real Estate News, March 10, 1978, for such a case.

58) Record, August, 13, 1897. Mueller in 'Onkel Karl' explains how he ordered the largest possible German flag from Hamburg. It arrived the afternoon of the unveiling and when run up the pole was many times the size of the British ensign, '...as a colorful handkerchief to the sail of the sailboat.'

59) Victoria Park Myth! The vandalism of the German flag before the war began is well-documented in newspapers of the day. A careful search of contemporary papers, documents and memoirs reveals no such similar attack on the Union Jack. It is inconceivable this would have been covered up completely. Yet the story has been reversed by some later writers such as Moyer in Kitchener: Yesterday Revisited as well as Martin and Segrave in City Parks of Canada. Interestingly, in the Record of October 4, 1966, an anonymous ex-member of the 118th Battalion claims to have been an unknown fourth man involved in the bust toppling. An outrage to the Union Jack is given as one of the group's motivations. His incorporation of a non-event puts his entire tale under suspicion... or he may simply have subconsciously invented his own internal myth based on stories he had heard, something not unknown in oral history research. The large German flag was stored with the bust in the Concordia Society's club rooms and disappeared on February 15, 1916.

60) Telegraph, April 11, 1916. Renbourn's official report would make interesting reading. The Ontario Fire Marshal's office in Toronto does not have records for that period.

61) KPL and VPHC. A silver-nitrate 30mm negative was given to the Record in the mid 1970s by William Musclow a long-time projectionist in the city and an ex-member of the 118th. The Record had it converted to a 16mm positive. In the 1980s I came across this 16mm copy at the Record and had it transferred to video at CKCO TV. Copies were provided for KPL and area high schools. A slightly different version is at National Archives, Ottawa.The quality is still excellent although there are several segments with severe jumping where frames had been taken out for copying. Earlier moving pictures were taken in Berlin (eg the 1910 Hydro Power ceremony) but they seem not to have survived. Charlie Roos went on to great fame in film-making throughout North America. For Roos' career, and a documentary on his life, see Record, September 18, 1987. His great-niece Barbara Boyden, is also a film-maker. Her 1987 documentary Those Roos Boys and Friends examines the suprising careers of Charlie and his brother Len. In this case the name is pronounced as in choose. For William Roos, the Park Board member after whom Roos Island is named, pronounce as in rose. The two familieswere not closely related.

62) CGC. September 17, 1917. Ada Clemens to Gordon Eby. Eby was an officer in the 118th and saw front-line service overseas. His wartime diaries are as yet unpublished but provide a fascinating look at a young man's rapid maturing in uniform. The collection of Eby's diaries, photographs, documents, memorabilia and family letters forms an extensive and valuable archive at Conrad Grebel College. Gordon Eby was a great grandson of one of Berlin's founders, Bishop Benjamin Eby.

63) Telegraph, August 6, 1918.

64) Telegraph, May 7, 1921. Others honoured included Nurse Edith Cavell, General James Wolfe, Egerton Ryerson & Queen Victoria. Homer Peguegnat named his memorial tree after principal Carmichael. Research might indicate Homer's grades that year!

65) Record, April 16 to 29, 1926. Numerous articles trace Koehler's accident, hospitalization, death and funeral. One of the disappointments in researching this book was not being able to find a verified photo of Koehler.

66) Record, April 29, 1926.

67) VPHC, oral history interview with Oscar Rieck by Sharon Kelly, July 29, 1993.

68) VPHC, oral history interview with Walter Bean by Sharon Kelly, November 28, 1993.

69) VPHC, oral history interview and letters with Eileen Quickfall Dahms by rych mills 1994.

70) WHSR, Volume 82. Kitchener: 1995. The author's 'Ice Harvesting in Victoria Park' goes into more detail on this early industry.

71) (Joseph Meyer Snyder) Hannes Schneider and His Wife Catherine Haus Schneider. A privately published historical compendium-cum-treasure trove that is, in effect, a life's work by a nephew of Samuel Schneider and son of David Schneider. Joseph M Snyder collected clippings, articles, interviews, documents, photographs, songs, anecdotes, essays and reports and published them under his daughter's name, Miriam Helen Snyder ( later Sokvitne). The book was meant mainly for family use but copies of it are in local libraries and archives. Much of the original material and photographs, including that left out of the final printing, has been deposited by Miriam Sokvitne in the Joseph Meyer Snyder Family Fonds at Conrad Grebel College, Waterloo. For swimming hole memories see this book on pages 13 (Joseph M Snyder); 115 and 120A (David Schneider); 307 (S W Jackson); 308 (J P Jaffray, who quotes Joseph E Schneider in the 1860s '...go to it boys, the water is warm.')

72) Telegraph, May 6, 1915.

73) Record, April 17, 1930. The Park Board recommends a Victoria Park site to council. A summer-ful of legal battles dragged on into the fall. The pool opened at Woodside in 1931. In 1992 it was renamed Harry Class Community Pool to honour a Kitchener swimming and diving champion whose career spanned that of the pool.

74) Telegraph and Record, June 27-July 8, 1921.

75) (anon.) Kitchener Musical Society Band Since 1876. An historical pamphlet (undated, 1960s). Information in this chapter also from interviews with long-time band member Vern Hett, conducted in the 1992-96 period.

76) Record, July 30, 1949. Frank Schantz was one of the city's keenest amateur naturalists. His brother Orpheus moved to Chicago but returned often to visit and took many photographs in Victoria Park. Frank and Orpheus were uncles to Dorothy Russell. Frank is also quoted by Uttley, p285, on bird species in Victoria Park, counting over 75.

77) Telegraph, June 10, 1898 (Refreshment Booth); Record, July 2, 1897 (Nails Sprinkled); Record, October 3, 1899 (Man Hugs); Telegraph, April 19, 1901 (Bicycle Stolen); Record, August 16, 1900 (Profanities);

78) Record. In the summer of 1984 police began videotaping the washrooms in Victoria Park and uncovered illegal homosexual acts. In December 1984, 45 year old Carl Schafer was knifed to death in the park. In June 1985 a minister was stabbed but not seriously injured. Shelly Lynn Ellison, a 23 year old university student, was murdered while jogging through the park in October 1985.

Note: All personal quotes in shaded boxes throughout the book are from oral history tapes in the VPHC archives.

# Bibliography

Publications with specific Victoria Park focus or essential to a study of the community. Items with * were of particular value.

Elizabeth Bloomfield. *Waterloo Township Through Two Centuries.* Kitchener: Waterloo Historical Society. 1995.*

Wendy Collishaw and Barry Preston, ed. *Recollections of 125 Years.* Kitchener: Committee for the 125th, 1979.

W R Chadwick. *The The Battle for Berlin, Ontario.* Waterloo: WLU Press, 1982.

Cindy Day. *Anti-German Sentiment in Berlin During the First World War.* Waterloo: University of Waterloo thesis, 1988.

E F Donohue, ed. *Kitchener Centennial 1854 - 1954.* Kitchener: Centennial Committee, 1954.

John English and Kenneth McLaughlin. *Kitchener: An Illustrated History.* Waterloo: Wilfrid Laurier Press, 1983.*

Otto Friedrich. *Blood and Iron: The von Moltke Family's Impact on German History.* New York: HarperCollins, 1995.

E Reginald Good. *Tour of Kitchener, Ontario: Featuring Sites of Aboriginal Historical Interest.* Kitchener: 1992. (pamphlet)

E Reginald Good. 'Mississauga - Mennonite Relations in the Upper Grand River Valley'. *Ontario History,* June 1995.*

Nicholas Hill. *Victoria Park Area Heritage Conservation District Study.* Kitchener: 1995.

Rev Peter Jones (Kahkewaquonaby.) *History of the Ojebway Indians: with Especial Reference to Their Conversion to Christianity.* London, England: A W Bennett, 1861*

Fred Landon and Jesse Edgar Middleton, ed. *The Province of Ontario.* Toronto: Dominion Publishing, 1927. 4 vols.*

Gottlieb Leibbrandt. *Little Paradise: The Saga of German Canadians of Waterloo County, Ontario.* Kitchener: Allprint,1980*

Linda Martin and Kerry Segrave. *City Parks of Canada.* Oakville: Mosaic Press, 1983.

Patricia McKegney. *The Kaiser's Bust: A Study of War-Time Propaganda in Berlin, Ontario 1914-18.* Bamberg: Bamberg Heritage Series, 1991.*

Bill Moyer. Kitchener: *Yesterday Revisited. An Illustrated History.* Burlington: Windsor Publications/Kitchener Chamber of Commerce, 1979.

James Nyce, ed. *The Gordon C Eby Diaries 1911-13: Chronicle of a Mennonite Farmer.* Toronto: Multicultural History Society, 1982.

Patti Shea. *Victoria Park: An Inventory of Historic Buildings.* Kitchener: Kitchener LACAC, 1988.

Donald Smith. *Sacred Feathers: The Reverend Peter Jones (Kakewaquonaby) and the Mississauga Indians.* Toronto: U of T Press, 1987.

(Joseph M Snyder, ed.) *Hannes Schneider and His Wife Catherine Haus Schneider Their Descendants and Times, 1534 - 1939.* Kitchener: 1939. (actually published in the mid 1940s).*

Edna Staebler. *Sauerkraut and Enterprise.* Toronto: McClelland and Stewart, 1973 (reprinted).

Ray Stanton. *Kitchener, a Tradition of Excellence: A Contemporary Portrait.* Windsor Publications, 1991.

W V Uttley. *A History of Kitchener, Ontario.* Waterloo : Chronicle Press, 1937.*

W V Uttley. *A History of Kitchener, Ontario.* Waterloo : WLU Press, 1975. reissued, intro. by Gerald Noonan.*

Philip Ziegler. *Mountbatten.* New York: Alfred Knopf, 1985.

Anon.
– *Souvenir of Victoria Park, Berlin Ontario.* Berlin: H S Hallman, 1901.*
– *20th Century Souvenir of Busy Berlin: The Best Town in Canada.* Berlin: Berlin News Record, 1901.
– *Berlin: Celebration of Cityhood 1912.* Berlin: German Printing and Publishing Company, 1912.
– *Berlin Canada: A Self-Portrait of Kitchener, Ontario Before World War One.* St. Jacobs: Sand Hills Press, 1979. *
  ed. and intro. by Paul Tiessen. Reproduction of previous item plus additional material.
– *Peace Souvenir: Activities of Waterloo County in the Great War 1914-18.* Kitchener Daily Telegraph. 1919.
– *Victoria Park: 90th Celebration 1896-1986 Souvenir.* Kitchener: 90th Birthday Committee. 1986.
– *K-W First Nations Cultural Pow-Wow.* Kitchener: 1994. Souvenir program with concise K-W First Nations history.

# Photograph and Illustration Credits

Copies of all photos and illustrations in this book are in the Victoria Park Historical Committee archives. The following are original sources. (T=top row M=middle row B=bottom row. i,ii,iii = numbered from left. D=donated to Victoria Park Historical Committee archives.)

Rosemary Aicher. IIITi

Annette Augustine. 67Tii

Berlin: Celebration of Cityhood, 1912. Berlin: German Printing and Publishing Company, 1912. 7B, 8B, 9Ti, 17Bi, 24ii, 34ii, 40B, 53Ti, 53Bii

Conrad Grebel College at the University of Waterloo maintains the Joseph Meyer Snyder Family Fonds, donated by Miriam (Snyder) Sokvitne. 41Bi, 77Ti, 80Ti

Gloria Deorksen. 14Ti, 75Bi

Margaret Farrow Collection includes photos taken by her grandfather W G Cleghorn and her father Albert Fuller. 21, 25i, 39, 42i, 43, 69Tii, 70Bii, 75Bii, 78Ti, IIBi

Lorna Ferguson. 68B, IVTi, IVB, Back Cover Bi

Murray Fried. 38Bii

Esther Gawlik. 69Bii

Rob Glover.19T, 70M

Lori Gove. 77Bi

Bruce Gress Collection includes photos taken by Annie Gress and Dolores (Syrotiuk) Gress. 45i, 69Tiii, IITii

Helga Hartman. 75Tiii

Vern Hett Collection includes many by others of various Kitchener Musical Society bands. 58i, 59Tii

Evelyn and Arthur Hewitt Collection also includes professional photographs of William B Hewitt's excavations.10,11,12,13T

John Johnston. 74Mi

Joseph Schneider Haus Archives.5i, 6i, 7Tii

Kitchener Local Architectural Conservation Advisory Committee (LACAC).34i

Kitchener Parks and Recreation: Chandler Drive Collection.9Bi, 9Bii

Kitchener Public Library's Collection at the Grace Schmidt Room of Local History.3(1881 Parsell map), 4Ti, 4Tii, 4Tiii, 20, 23i, 37, 40Ti, 79T

Leah Kruse Collection includes photos by other family members.33Tii, 76Tii

Heather Lackner.53Tii

Lippert Family Collection includes photographs taken by George Lippert and Ellroy Lippert. 40Tii, 72Mii, IIBii

Dilys Miehm. 87

Anne Millar Collection includes photographs taken by her father Gordon Eby.24i

Mills Family Collection includes photos taken by Robert, Dorothy, Fred, and Betty Mills. 69Ti

rych mills collection contains photos taken by the author and an extensive poscard archive. 2, 4B, 5ii (1875 : G H Yost, Pub), 25iii, 27B, 29M, 30B, 31T, 31B, 33Ti, 42ii, 48B, 50Ti, 50Tii, 55M, 58ii, 61i, 72Bii, 73M, 74Tii, 74B, 77Tii, 77Bii,ITi, ITii, IITi, IIITii, IIIBi, IIIBii, IVTii, Back Cover Ti, Tii, Bii

Dave and Sandy Moore. 18i

Roy and Cecile Musselman. 70Bi

National Archives of Canada, Ottawa.79Bi

Lynda O'Krafka.26, 67Bi

Ruth Otterbein. 47

Patricia Perrett. IBi

Neil Petersen / Eric Praetzel. 80Bii

Mark Peterson. 82, 83

Petsche Family Collection. 76Tiii, 76Bii

Joe Potje Collection includes photos by Matt Potje Sr and others.17Bii, 45ii, 73Bi

Quickfall Family Collection includes photos provided by Eileen Dahms and Peggy Kraemer. 51B, 52T

Eleanor Rau. 73Ti

Kitchener-Waterloo Record Historical Photograph Collection maintained at the Record's Fairway Road offices. 23iii(FEDNEWS), 35ii, 38Ti, 38Tii, 41T, 41Bii, 44,48T, 54i, 56, 67M, 70Ti, 70Tii, 70Bi, 71Ti, 71Tii, 71Bii, 74Mii, 79Bii

June and Robert Rieck Collection includes photos taken by several family members. 46, 62ii, 72Ti

Dorothy Russell Collection includes photos taken by her and several other Schantz and Russell family members. 14Ti, 14B, 17T, 27M, 29T, 29B, 32Ti, 32Tii, 32Bii, 33B, 35i, 40M, 52B, 55T, 67Ti, 68Ti, 69Bii, 74Ti, 75Ti, 76Ti, 76Bi, 78M, 78B, 80Tii, 80Bi, 90

Herb and Betty Schneider Collection also includes several photos by, and of, unknown people in Victoria Park. 18ii, 22i

Miriam (Snyder) Sokvitne Collection includes photos taken by Josph Meyer Snyder, Albert Snyder and other Snyder/Schneider family members. 7Ti, 13Bii-D, 15Ti-D, 15B-D, 22ii, 32Bi-D, 36, 69Bi

Souvenir of Victoria Park, Berlin, Ontario. Berlin H S Hallman, 1901. 8Ti, 8Tii

20th Century Souvenir of Busy Berlin: The Best Town in Canada. Berlin: Berlin News Record, 1901. 51T, 64

University of Waterloo Library's Doris Lewis Rare Book Room contains several Special Collections utilized in this publication, viz:

    1) The Kitchener-Waterloo Record's Historical Negative Collection. 28, 30T, 38M, 38Bi, 49, 50Bi, 50Bii, 53Bi, 54ii, 55B, 57ii, 59B, 60ii, 62i,67Bii, 68Tii, 71Bi, 72Tii, 72Mi, 72Bi, 73Tii,73Bii

    2) The YWCA of Kitchener-Waterloo Collection. 25ii

    3) The Breithaupt Family Papers in the Breithaupt Hewetson Clark Collection. 19B

University of Waterloo Library. 6ii (1854 Schofield map),

Victoria Park Historical Committee Archives.15Ti

Waterloo Historical Society Collection, located at Kitchener Public Library's Grace Schmidt Room. 23ii, 27T, 57i

Paul Widmeyer. 61ii

Bert Williams.60i

John and Cora Ziegler. 59Ti

# Acknowledgements

*by rych mills*

Although my name appears on the cover and various other places in this book, it wouldn't be there without the assistance, guidance and encouragement of hundreds of other people. From the beginning of this project there has been a solid core of support and along the way many others have lent their expertise.

*First,* to the other members of the Victoria Park 100th Birthday Historical Committee, there isn't a font big enough to print my THANK-YOU! All those meetings, all those early morning display set-ups and evening teardowns, all those malls, Multicultural Festivals, Plowing Matches, all that keyboarding...it's all been worth it! Johanna Jamnik, Dorothy Russell, Nancy Zurbrigg, Lynda O'Krafka, Harold Russell, Miriam Sokvitne, Lorna Ferguson, Kathryn Lamb, Whitney Densmore, Glennis and Mark Yantzi, Marion Heath, Sharon Kelly, Helen Warner and Lee Stones. I could write a chapter on each one's contributions.

*Second,* Kitchener Parks and Recreation. From the corner office on the 7th floor of City Hall to the park caretakers they have unfailingly put up with my questions, ideas, requests and complaints. Thank you Tom Clancy, general manager, for being more than a manager, for having a feeling for the history of Victoria Park. Current Parks and Recreation people such as Dan Daly, Ted Potworka and Rob Nuhn deserve much credit. Henry Eckert (just recently retired) and the late Ken Shiry lent their many years of park recollections.

*Third,* the professional local history people have opened their archives, shared their expertise and given much encouragement. Susan Hoffman of Kitchener Public Library's Grace Schmidt Room, Susan Burke of Joseph Schneider Haus, Susan Saunders Bellingham at the University of Waterloo's Special Collections Library, Sandra Woolfrey at Wilfred Laurier University and Lynn Boland Richardson at the Kitchener-Waterloo Record, thank-you

*Fourth,* the contributors who lent us their photo albums, their family's memories and patiently answered all the questions. Many thanks to Garry Steffler (K-W Sea Cadets), Vern Hett (Kitchener Musical Society), Lucile Rieck, Evelyn Hahn, Annette Augustine, Renie Rumpel, Bill and Leah Kruse, Herb and Betty Schneider, Rob Glover, Evelyn and Arthur Hewitt, June and Robert Rieck, Dave and Sandy Moore, Dr John and Cora Ziegler, Joseph Edward Snyder, Eileen Dahms, Peggy Kraemer and Dilys Miehm. Margaret Farrow patiently opened up all her family photo albums and boxes, and what a treasure trove! Walter Bean gave us his memories of Victoria Park and contributed in a material way to ensure this book's publication: thank you Walter. Joe Potje, like the author, had a special family connection to Victoria Park. I was honoured to work with Joe and Twin City Dwyer Printing Co. Ltd. on this publication.

*Fifth,* along the way a number of professionals in associated fields came to the fore to assist in getting this book off the ground. I have been fortunate to call Brian Clark a friend for nearly 30 years. I tested that friendship severely during the preparation of this book, but Brian and the Kitchener-Waterloo Record came through every time. Another Brian, Brian McHugh of Elmira Photo Works, assisted greatly in photographic work. The now-retired Don Willcox of CKCO TV put some of that station's resources at our disposal in the early years of research. Chris Schooley of Rogers Cable produced a still-seen profile of Victoria Park. Elin Edwards with her quarterly tabloid, Waterloo County Times, has helped spread the story of Victoria Park throughout the region. Mark Peterson took a hand-scrawled map of the park and turned out the concise and precise edition contained in the book

*Sixth,* special thanks to Doug and Peter Etril Snyder. In addition to the cover painting, the Snyders donated a portion of their print sales to the publication of the book. Also special thanks to Virgil Martin and all members of Waterloo Regional Heritage Foundation whose support made this book possible. Sincere appreciation to Alice Gastmeier for a contribution and Lynda O'Krafka for picture-finding and problem-solving.

*Seventh,* Geertje Gubitz provided a sparkling translation of the idiosyncratic memoirs of a bitter Karl Mueller. Nicholas Hill and Margaret Goodbody, while working on the Victoria Park Heritage District project, fell in love with the park and we would be poorer without their professional examination of the area. Don Pullen needed all his many years of teaching English to rein in some of my grammatical whimsies. His brand of non-dogmatic grammar provided a comfortable working envelope. Reg Good started as a voice on the phone at Conrad Grebel College and ended up as someone I could depend and call upon. His encouragement was welcome more than once!

*Eighth,* Ryan Taylor. Kitchener lost a valuable historical presence when Ryan moved to the United States. I didn't. Ryan's assistance transcended friendship and saved me from several historical howlers which would have blighted the book.

*Ninth,* in the final shaping of this book the author and committee were in trouble until Lisa Schropp arrived with her expertise in computer layout technology. The look of this book is as good as it is thanks to Lisa.

*Tenth,* There is no official dedication of this book but the author's very special tip-of-the-hat goes to his uncle, Bruce Gress. As the photo in the book attests, he and I go back a long way in Victoria Park. With my continual questions about "How Things Were" his memory has had to work overtime. Following in his father's footsteps, Bruce's recent retirement gave the Gress clan 70-plus consecutive years of service to Victoria Park and the Kitchener Parks Department.

*Eleventh,* within any list of acknowledgements one must somehow express in words a level of Thank Yous and Appreciations which transcends the written word. I get a headache just thinking of the number of hours Whitney Densmore spent in front of her monitor inputting my (poorly) typed and white-outed drafts. From Day One, Lorna Ferguson was the engineer of this train which has resulted in the book you are holding. At some junctions it threatened to jump the tracks when others touched the throttle, but she kept it on course with wise counsel and much (extra)ordinary hard work. I cannot envision the publication which would have resulted without her advice and assistance.

*Twelfth,* to those I have leaned on in the development of this book but not named, please blame faulty memory not lack of appreciation. This "Thank's" for you.

*Final Author's Note.* You will have noticed the name Dorothy Russell throughout this book. Without Dorothy, this would have been a much poorer production. Born in 1900, during the reign of the park's namesake, she began photographing Victoria Park in 1910 and seems to have never stopped. Several other members of the Moyer-Schantz-White-Russell family were avid snapshotters and many of their views have ended up in Dorothy's collection. When the Victoria Park 100th Birthday Historical Committee archives were just starting, some 200 park photos from the Dorothy Russell albums gave it a jump start. Unfailingly coming out to our historical displays and standing for hours talking history, Dorothy's cheerfulness has been a constant spirit-lifter and inspiration for all members of the committee.